LONDON
# Like a Local

# LONDON
# Like a Local

## BY THE PEOPLE WHO CALL IT HOME

# Contents

## NIGHTLIFE

## OUTDOORS

# meet the locals

### FLORENCE DERRICK

*Florence moved to London to kick-start her career in journalism. Though her writing takes her all over the world, it's East London that she knows like the back of her hand. Outside of eating, drinking and dancing – in the name of journalism – Florence is sipping flat whites, browsing charity shops and researching gig tickets.*

### MARLENE LANDU

*Financial advisor Marlene arrived in London more than ten years ago and doesn't plan on leaving any time soon. The old 9–5 job aside, she loves to practise her downward dog, amble along Broadway Market and dish out restaurant recommendations to her friends (she seriously knows her stuff).*

### OLIVIA PASS

*Born in London, Olivia spent years in Hong Kong, which gave her a lifelong travel bug. When she's not working as a photographer and writer, Olivia is cycling between bakeries in search of London's perfect brownie, rambling through Dulwich Park with her husband and dog or enjoying a wild swim.*

# **London**

## WELCOME TO THE CITY

There are countless types of Londoner: long-time market traders whose roots run deep; recent graduates lured by the buzz; generations of immigrants who've breathed new life into the city. Yet what unites them all is the fact that – first and foremost – they are Londoners. Yes, they moan about overcrowded Tubes and eye-watering rent, but deep down they know that their home is like no other. It's a place with a fierce spirit, an engrained Blitz-like mentality that keeps soldiering on. Start-ups have sprouted in cracks caused by financial crisis, peaceful protests have given voice to all and communities have pulled together through thick and thin.

Think of London and you'll probably picture its iconic façade: majestic bridges lacing the Thames, the riverbanks sown with gleaming skyscrapers and historic landmarks. But famous sights aside, London is, at its core, a place where people live – a tapestry of distinctive neighbourhoods, woven with Victorian terraces and tower blocks, and punctuated by well-trodden parks and beloved boozers. It's in these neighbourhood communities that London is at its most real, and its most exciting.

London can be an overwhelming place but that's where this book comes in. We know the places that Londoners love, from just whispered-about restaurants to underground venues that nurture old and new talent. Of course, with nearly 9 million citizens, there are more Londoners than these pages can do justice to. Instead, this book celebrates snapshots of local life in a city that's as diverse as its inhabitants.

Whether you're a restless Londoner hungry to find the places that aren't on everyone else's radar, or a visitor looking to delve beyond the city's icons, this book will help you embrace a lesser-known London. So tear up the traditional bucket list, and enjoy London the local way.

## Liked by the locals

**"Sure, London can be exhausting. It constantly badgers you to keep up, teasing you with the constant gamble of what to do, and what to miss. But that's what I love most about London – you can never get bored."**

OLIVIA PASS,
PHOTOGRAPHER AND TRAVEL WRITER

*London takes on different personalities during each of the seasons. Think jubilant festivals in summer, cosy pub lunches in autumn and festive fun in winter.*

# London
## THROUGH THE YEAR

## SPRING

### RIVERSIDE EXPLORATION
As life unfurls after winter, Londoners inch outdoors to walk along the Thames path and cycle beside barge-dotted canals that snake around the city.

### MARKETS GALORE
Locals embrace the milder weather by migrating to the city's outdoor markets. They gather blooms on Columbia Road (p104), guzzle snacks at the Scandinavian Spring market and hunt for vintage treasures on Portobello Road (p89).

### OUTDOOR CINEMAS
From May onwards, open-air cinemas spring up across the city. Classic films are enjoyed with blankets, deck chairs and cocktails. The most spectacular is Secret Cinema, an immersive cinematic experience held in a secret location.

## SUMMER

### FESTIVAL FUN
Nothing brings Londoners together like its summer festival season. Pride in July and Notting Hill Carnival in August are joyous cultural celebrations, while the abundant music festivals – All Points East, Lovebox, Wireless and South West Four, to name but a few – draw fans from all corners of the city.

### WONDERFUL WIMBLEDON
Queueing at the crack of dawn for tickets to this famous tournament is a rite of passage for many locals. Those

less keen on an early wake-up call head to the big screens at Granary Square or St Katharine Docks instead.

## PARKS AND PICNICS

As temperatures rise, Londoners descend on the city's parks and gardens to celebrate the warm weather. Dog walkers stop to chat, families throw frisbees and friends toast the summer.

# AUTUMN

## CULTURAL TOURS

With the days cooling off, Londoners head indoors for a dose of culture. The curious join guided tours around private houses as part of September's Open House Festival and enjoy events during October's Museums at Night weekend.

## WEEKEND ROASTS

On a cold and rainy weekend there's one place Londoners are guaranteed to gather: a cosy pub serving slap-up roasts with all the trimmings.

## FIREWORKS FOR DAYS

London's fireworks season begins with Bonfire Night on 5 November and continues into Diwali in mid-November.

Most weekends include a dazzling display of fireworks, sparklers and locals cocooned in coats in the city's parks.

# WINTER

## CHRISTMAS IN THE CITY

Festive markets and ice rinks pop up across the city, the city centre is strung with lights and mulled wine is added to pub menus. It's the same every year and yet locals still lap it all up.

## JOLLY JUMPERS

Londoners love a festive jumper – the more garish, the better – and most of London's Christmas parties entail wearing a brightly patterned knit.

## NEW YEAR'S EVE

While some Londoners seek a riverside spot to watch the New Year's Eve fireworks over the Thames, most prefer to watch the show on the TV with a glass of champers and their loved ones.

## DRY JANUARY

Tired and broke after Christmas, Londoners often promise they won't drink in January. But a few weeks into the year and most ask their friends, "pub?"

*There's an art to being a Londoner, from the dos and don'ts in the pub to negotiating the city's intricate streets. Here's a breakdown of all you need to know.*

# London
## KNOW-HOW

For a directory of health and safety resources, safe spaces and accessibility information, turn to page 190. For everything else, read on.

## EAT
Londoners will find any excuse to eat out. Weekends revolve around leisurely brunches and roasts, with restaurants and pubs starting to fill up from 11am. Dinner is the main meal of the day and starts any time from 7 or 8pm. It's a good idea to book a table wherever possible, though some hotspots don't take reservations. They'll instead ask for your number on arrival and text you when your table is ready, so you can nip off for a drink.

## DRINK
Pubs are so much more than places to drink; they're social institutions. Our tips? Make sure you buy a "round" – a drink for each person in your group – and wait your turn at the bar (one of the few places that locals don't queue, but it's still polite). Last orders are at 10:45pm, when a bell is rung as a prompt; the bar closes at 11pm.

Londoners are fuelled by coffee and largely drink it from takeaway cups, en route to work or in the park with friends. Some coffee shops offer a discount if you bring a reusable cup.

## SHOP
Londoners tend to avoid Oxford Street, preferring to shop on their local high streets, which have a mix of chain stores and independents. Shops are generally open from 9am to 5:30pm, though they often close earlier on Sundays. Markets are usually held on weekends only and, these days, haggling isn't really the done thing. It's always worth carrying a tote bag to avoid the charge for a plastic one.

## ARTS & CULTURE

London's big museums and galleries are, wonderfully, free to enter, though you do need to buy tickets to temporary exhibitions. Popular theatre shows can be pricey and need to be booked well in advance but box offices do last-minute deals. Performances usually start around 7pm and round off by 11pm. It's all very casual these days so you don't need to dress up (unless you want to, of course).

## NIGHTLIFE

Nights out in London generally start in the pub, or with "pre-drinks" at home, if the plan is to hit a club later. Doors open at clubs and music venues around 7pm but things don't really get started until 9 or 10pm. Lots of bars and pubs turn into dance venues around 10pm, too, with tables getting pushed to the side. When it comes to what to wear, again, you don't need to dress up. Just be sure to have your ID on you – security at the door nearly always ask, however old you look.

## OUTDOORS

On a sunny day, Londoners flock to the city's parks for picnics and catch-ups. Here there are countless recycling and rubbish bins, so do your bit to help look after these green spaces. There's a big homeless population in London, so it's not unheard of to be approached for food in the city's parks. The canal tow paths make for a lovely stroll but note walkers share the narrow paths with cyclists.

# Keep in mind

**Here are some more tips and tidbits that will help you fit in like a local.**

» **Contactless** The majority of places take card – you can even use it at street food venues, and to tap on and off the Underground.

» **No smoking** Lighting up is a definite no-no in all indoor spaces. If you have to smoke, do so in a designated spot outside.

» **Tipping** A tip of 10 or 12.5 per cent is the norm in restaurants, with some places adding it to the bill as a matter of course.

» **Stay hydrated** London is home to lots of free drinking fountains, so bring a bottle. You can also ask bartenders to refill it for you.

## GETTING AROUND

London is made up of 12 inner boroughs and 20 outer boroughs, each of which comprise a handful of neighbourhoods (p14). Generally speaking, though, locals think of London both physically and culturally as five distinct areas – central, north, south, east and west, with the Thames running through the city's heart. Postcodes also reflect these areas and are included on many street signs (SW, for example, refers to neighbour-hoods south and then west of central), which can help you navigate your way around the city. Most locals live outside of central London.

To make your life easier we've provided what3words addresses for each sight in this book, meaning you can quickly pinpoint exactly where you're heading with ease.

### On foot

London is so well served by the Underground that it's easy to forget how walkable the city is. It's not uncommon for Londoners to get off the Tube a stop early and walk the last leg of their journey, especially if it means avoiding a notoriously crowded station (Oxford Circus: we're looking at you). Besides which, walking is the best way to see the city in all its glory. Having said this,

Londoners are very fast walkers so don't dawdle in the middle of the pavement. If you do need to stop and check a what3words location, step to the side so that people can pass.

### On wheels

This is a city of keen cyclists and so the cycle lane network is constantly being improved. Hitting central London on two wheels can be a little daunting so try and stick to other cyclists if you can. Watch out for pedestrians crossing the road, never go through a red light (even if you see your fellow cyclists doing it) and try not to cycle too close to the curb – it gives drivers the impression that they can get past you, even if there's not enough room. Finally, always wear a helmet. No arguments.

Visitors can use the public bicycle scheme, Santander Cycles, which has over 750 docking stations across London. You can hire them via the official app or by using your bank card at one of the docking stations. It costs £2 to access a bike for 24 hours, with the first 30 minutes of each journey free. Note that the legal drink-drive limit (50 mg of alcohol per 100 ml of blood, equivalent to a small glass of wine or a pint of lager) also applies to cyclists. *www.santandercycles.co.uk*

## By public transport

London's transport network, which is run by Transport for London (TfL), includes the Underground (or "the Tube"), buses, Overground, and the Docklands Light Railway (DLR). National Rail looks after the trains running in and out of the city.

Once you've learned the basics of the Underground, it's easy to navigate. In short, Tube lines are colour-coded and trains travel in two directions: north and south, or east and west. Always stand on the right when you're on an escalator going down to the Tube, move well inside the Tube train carriage, and be ready to give up your seat to anyone in need. Alternatively, you can catch a bus but be prepared to face the city's traffic. If you're escaping the city for the day, note that train fares are cheaper outside of peak hours (6:30–9:30am and 4–7pm). *www.nationalrail.co.uk*

## By car or taxi

Londoners don't tend to drive. There's an off-putting daily fee of £15 for cars entering the central Congestion Zone plus all-round horrendous traffic. Now and then they use taxis, like the iconic black cabs, which can be hailed on the street in central London or booked with the Gett Taxi app. For cheaper fares, they prefer the likes of Uber, Bolt and Ola.

# Download these

We recommend you download these apps to help you get about the city.

### WHAT3WORDS
**Your geocoding friend**

A what3words address is a simple way to communicate any precise location on earth, using just three words. ///pipes.actor.bossy, for example, is the code for the David Bowie mural in Brixton. Simply download the free what3words app, type a what3words address into the search bar, and you'll know exactly where to go.

### TFL
**Your local transport service**

The app from Transport for London lays out all your best options for moving around the city, as well as live departures and delay information for each stop. It's a great source for checking when the last train or bus is, too, so you don't miss either.

*London is a city of cities and every neighbourhood has its own wonderful flavour and community. Here we take a look at some of our favourites.*

# London
## NEIGHBOURHOODS

### Bermondsey

Once a centre of industry, Bermondsey is known for its enviable warehouse flats, world-class restaurant scene and craft breweries, which culminate in the Bermondsey Beer Mile. {map 5}

### Bethnal Green

Old East End flavour lives on here, with stalwarts like Columbia Road Flower Market giving a window to the past. Shabby-chic spaces now house bougie bars and restaurants, tempting young professionals to put down roots in the area. {map 2}

### Brixton

Historically a multiethnic area, with a strong Afro-Caribbean community,

Brixton has seen contentious gentrification. Having said that, it's still hard to beat for powerful street art and buzzing markets. {map 5}

### Camden

Famed for its counterculture, Camden was at the heart of the punk rock movement in the 70s, and Britpop in the mid-90s. Music lovers still journey across the city for a gig here, ideally after a few hours sat by the Regent's Canal or a bite at Camden Market. {map 1}

### Clerkenwell

Though calm in the day, creative Clerkenwell comes alive at night as office workers stream into its pubs, bars and restaurants. {map 1}

### Covent Garden

Londoners might not live in this historic shopping district but they do pop by, weaving around tourists and street performers to pick up coffee and run their day's errands. {map 1}

### Fulham

Largely home to the high-earning, Fulham is quiet during the week. But come the weekend, groups of friends pour into the area's cafés for brunch, families enjoy scenic riverside walks and football fans arrive for the beautiful game. {map 4}

### Greenwich

When Londoners want to escape the city, they retreat to genteel Greenwich. Aside from its clutch of pubs and shops, Greenwich has grand naval buildings and a sprawling park – the perfect backdrop for picnics. {map 6}

## Hackney

Forget Shoreditch; Hackney is the real hipster's paradise. Edgy and innovative, the area is awash with craft breweries, artisan bakeries and street art, not forgetting a glut of street food and vintage markets. {map 3}

## Islington

Grand townhouses, chi-chi boutiques and top-quality restaurants have long attracted liberal elites to this part of the city. But it's not all champagne socialism. In Angel, the area's heart, down-to-earth comedy clubs and music venues keep the masses entertained. {map 2}

## Kensington

Visitors flock to stately Kensington for the Natural History Museum, Science Museum and V&A. Affluent locals stay on for the posh dining spots and top-notch shopping. {map 4}

## Notting Hill

Forget what you saw on the big screen: Notting Hill is as diverse as they come, with pastel-hued houses over-looked by tower blocks and its backstreets lined with assorted restaurants. This is also the home of the city's most joyous carnival. {map 4}

## Nunhead

A stone's throw from trendy Peckham is sleepy Nunhead. The area flies under the radar despite its community-minded shops and lovely green spaces. {map 5}

## Peckham

Sorry, Brixton, but it's all about Peckham these days. It's buzzy, multicultural and fast becoming a foodie destination. Creatives also love the area for its uber-cool arts spaces. {map 5}

## Shoreditch

This was the heartland of alternative east London in the 90s, though it's done up to the nines these days. That said, Shoreditch remains a heartland for creatives and foodies. {map 2}

## Soho

Sex shops hark back to Soho's history as London's red light district but today the area is better known for its LGBTQ+ nightlife and fab dining scene. {map 1}

## South Bank

This cultural hub is a local icon. Londoners might not live here but they regularly attend performances at the Southbank Centre, or sip evening drinks beside the river and take in the view of the London Eye and Houses of Parliament. {map 5}

## Spitalfields

Old meets new in Spitalfields and nearby Brick Lane, both areas of past immigration that now tempt Londoners to their fancy precincts, vintage markets and curry houses. {map 2}

## Stoke Newington

Fast gentrifying but still genuinely multicultural, with a strong Jewish community, Stokey is loved for its indie shops, brunch spots and village feel. {map 3}

# London
## ON THE MAP

*Whether you're looking for your new favourite spot or want to check out what each part of London has to offer, our maps – along with handy map references throughout the book – have you covered.*

6

EDGWARE

COLINDALE

HENDON

HARROW

WEMBLEY

WILLESDEN

EALING

ACTON

HAYES

SOUTHALL

WEST DRAYTON

BRENTFORD

KEW
Kew Gardens

BARNES

HEATHROW

HOUNSLOW

RICHMOND

TWICKENHAM

Richmond Park

FELTHAM

HAM

Wimbledon Common

STAINES

ASHFORD

SUNBURY

Bushy Park

MOLESEY

KINGSTON-UPON THAMES

River Thames

CHERTSEY

WALTON-ON THAMES

0 kilometres    4

0 miles    4

ESHER

EWELL

Roundhouse **N**

**E** **E** Rudy's Vegan Diner

Cheese Bar **S** Camden Market

Paddleboard on **O**
Regent's Canal

**A** Kentish Town Road

CAMDEN

CAMDEN RD

Regent's Canal

BARNSBURY

YORK WAY

CALEDONIAN ROAD

Jazz Cafe **N**

The Jewish Museum **A**

ALBANY STREET

CAMDEN HIGH ST

EVERSHOLT STREET

Spiritland **D**

The Coal Office **E**

**S** Word on the Water

KING'S CROSS

The Story **O**
Garden

EUSTON ROAD

PENTONVILLE ROAD

**D** Big Chill House

Regent's Park

The Crypt Gallery **A**

EUSTON ROAD

MARYLEBONE ROAD

**S** The Conran Shop

MARYLEBONE

**S** Daunt Books

TOTTENHAM COURT ROAD

GOWER STREET

WOBURN PLACE

**S** Gay's The Word

Coram's Fields

Russell Square

BLOOMSBURY

British Museum **A**

GRAY'S INN ROAD

**A** The Postal Museum

THEOBALD'S ROAD

Gray's Inn

HOLBORN

**N** All Star Lanes

**E** Rovi

Omotesando **D** Koffee

**N** Flight Club

Lincoln's Inn Fields

Workshop **D**
Coffee

OXFORD STREET

The Photographers' Gallery

OXFORD STREET

Cavendish Square

Reckless Records **E**

Phonica **S**

She Soho **N**

Bao **E** **E**

Temper

Kiln **E**

Yauatcha **E**

SOHO

Freud **D**

Monmouth Coffee

COVENT GARDEN

Redemption Bar **D**

**E** **D** The Barbary

**E** Seven Dials Market

**S** Stanfords

KINGSWAY

**A** 180 The Strand

REGENT STREET

SHAFTESBURY AVENUE

CHARING CROSS RD

The Crystal Maze **N**
LIVE Experience

LEICESTER SQUARE

PICCADILLY CIRCUS

**E** Floral by Lima

COVENT GARDEN

**A** London Transport Museum

STRAND

VICTORIA EMBANKMENT

Waterloo Bridge

MAYFAIR

Grosvenor Square

0 metres 500
0 yards 500

PICCADILLY

National Gallery **A**

TRAFALGAR SQUARE

**D** The Harp

MAP 1

**The Albion**
**D**

ISLINGTON

**O** Culpeper
Community Garden

Sadler's
Wells **N**

CLERKENWELL

**E** Exmouth Market
**E** Caravan

FARRINGDON

ROAD

HOLBORN

Ye Olde
Cheshire Cheese
**D**
FLEET STREET

Blackfriars
Thames    Bridge

SOUTH BANK

UPPER STREET

**1**

**DALSTON**

0 metres 500
0 yards 500

UPPER STREET

ESSEX ROAD

S Flashback Records
Lucky Chip E
D N The Bill Murray
69 Colebrooke Row
S Annie's

**ISLINGTON**

Regent's Canal

NEW NORTH ROAD

Shoreditch Park

The Glory N
Gin House Burlesque N

CITY ROAD

Regent's Canal

KINGSLAND ROAD

**HAGGERSTON**

Haggerston Park

HACKNEY ROAD

Hackney City Farm O

The Royal Oak D S Columbia Road Flower Market

**HOXTON**

Modern Calligraphy at A Vintage Heaven
Bethnal Green N Working Men's Club

BETHNAL GREEN

**FINSBURY**

Rivington Street
A
S House of Hackney

Neon Naked Life Drawing

N A GREAT EASTERN ST N Ballie Ballerson
XOYO
E Nobu

OLD STREET

Bunhill Fields O Burial Ground

**SHOREDITCH**

Village Underground
N Boxpark

Queen of Hoxton D
Rough Trade East
A Brick Lane

CITY ROAD

Junkyard Golf Club N

S Brick Lane Vintage Market

**FARRINGDON**

Dennis Severs' House A
E St John Bread & Wine

S Old Spitalfields Market
**SPITALFIELDS**

N Barbican Centre

Eataly S N Gunpowder E D Pangea Café

S Smithfields Meat Market

LONDON WALL

Unity Diner E

BISHOPSGATE

COMMERCIAL STREET

WHITECHAPEL

HOLBORN

CHEAPSIDE

ALDGATE

LEMAN ST

**CITY OF LONDON**

CANNON ST

Wilton's Music Hall N

UPPER THAMES STREET

Mudlarking on O the North Bank

Blackfriars Bridge

Southwark Bridge

London Bridge

Thames

TOWER HILL

A Black History Walk

**SOUTHWARK**

MAP 2

HACKNEY

London
Fields

**2**

Bistrotheque **E**

CAMBRIDGE
HEATH

Phytology
Medicinal Garden **O**

Renegade
London Winery
ROAD **D**
**E** G Kelly

BETHNAL
GREEN

WHITECHAPEL
ROAD

**E** Lahore
Kebab House

SHADWELL

THE HIGHWAY

WAPPING

## **E** EAT

Bistrotheque *(p35)*

G Kelly *(p49)*

Gunpowder *(p52)*

Lahore Kebab House *(p51)*

Lucky Chip *(p51)*

Nobu *(p36)*

St John Bread & Wine *(p33)*

Unity Diner *(p46)*

## **D** DRINK

69 Colebrooke Row *(p65)*

Pangea Café *(p61)*

Queen of Hoxton *(p72)*

Renegade London Winery *(p83)*

The Royal Oak *(p76)*

## **S** SHOP

Annie's *(p91)*

Brick Lane Vintage Market *(p91)*

Columbia Road Flower Market *(p104)*

Flashback Records *(p94)*

House of Hackney *(p101)*

Rough Trade East *(p93)*

Old Spitalfields Market *(p88)*

Smithfields Meat Market *(p105)*

## **A** ARTS & CULTURE

Black History Walk *(p115)*

Brick Lane *(p117)*

Dennis Severs' House *(p114)*

Modern Calligraphy at Vintage Heaven *(p129)*

Neon Naked Life Drawing *(p131)*

Rivington Street *(p116)*

## **N** NIGHTLIFE

Ballie Ballerson *(p141)*

Barbican Centre *(p148)*

Bethnal Green Working Men's Club *(p151)*

The Bill Murray *(p149)*

Boxpark *(p138)*

Eataly *(p139)*

Gin House Burlesque *(p151)*

The Glory *(p156)*

Junkyard Golf Club *(p143)*

Village Underground *(p147)*

Wilton's Music Hall *(p148)*

XOYO *(p152)*

## **O** OUTDOORS

Bunhill Fields Burial Ground *(p177)*

Hackney City Farm *(p182)*

Mudlarking on the North Bank *(p175)*

Phytology Medicinal Garden *(p180)*

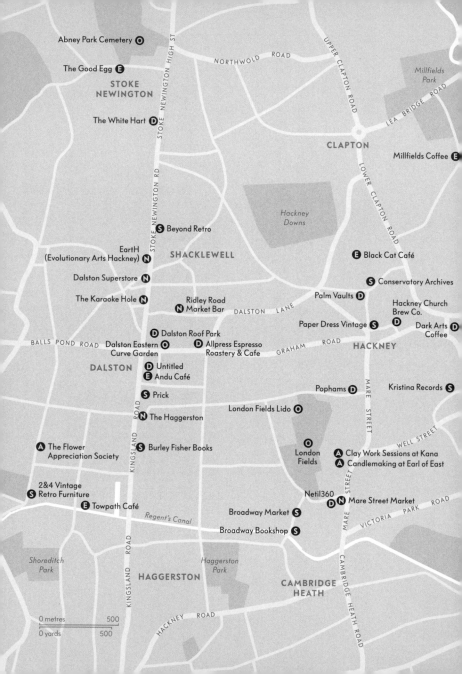

Abney Park Cemetery Ⓞ

The Good Egg Ⓔ

**STOKE
NEWINGTON**

NORTHWOLD ROAD

STOKE NEWINGTON HIGH ST

UPPER CLAPTON ROAD

*Millfields
Park*

LEA BRIDGE ROAD

The White Hart Ⓓ

STOKE NEWINGTON RD

**CLAPTON**

Millfields Coffee Ⓔ

LOWER CLAPTON ROAD

*Hackney
Downs*

Beyond Retro Ⓢ

**SHACKLEWELL**

Black Cat Café Ⓔ

EartH
(Evolutionary Arts Hackney) Ⓝ

Dalston Superstore Ⓝ

Conservatory Archives Ⓢ

The Karaoke Hole Ⓝ

Ridley Road Ⓝ
Market Bar

Palm Vaults Ⓓ

Hackney Church
Brew Co.

DALSTON LANE

Paper Dress Vintage Ⓢ

Dark Arts Ⓓ
Coffee

Dalston Roof Park Ⓓ

BALLS POND ROAD

Dalston Eastern Ⓞ
Curve Garden

Allpress Espresso Ⓓ
Roastery & Cafe

GRAHAM ROAD

**HACKNEY**

**DALSTON**

Untitled Ⓓ
Andu Café Ⓔ

Pophams Ⓓ

Kristina Records Ⓢ

Prick Ⓢ

London Fields Lido Ⓞ

KINGSLAND ROAD

MARE STREET

The Haggerston Ⓝ

The Flower Ⓐ
Appreciation Society

Burley Fisher Books Ⓢ

London Ⓞ
Fields

Clay Work Sessions at Kana Ⓐ
Candlemaking at Earl of East Ⓐ

WELL STREET

2&4 Vintage Ⓢ
Retro Furniture

Netil360 Ⓞ

Mare Street Market Ⓝ

Towpath Café Ⓔ

*Regent's Canal*

Broadway Market Ⓢ

MARE STREET

VICTORIA PARK ROAD

Broadway Bookshop Ⓢ

*Shoreditch
Park*

*Haggerston
Park*

**HAGGERSTON**

**CAMBRIDGE
HEATH**

KINGSLAND ROAD

CAMBRIDGE HEATH ROAD

0 metres          500

0 yards           500

HACKNEY ROAD

MAP 3

**3**

CLAPTON PARK

HOMERTON

HOMERTON HIGH ST

**The Spread Eagle** Ⓔ

CASSLAND ROAD

**People's Park Tavern** Ⓓ

**Victoria Park** Ⓞ

GROVE ROAD

**East London Liquor Company** Ⓓ

**The Palm Tree** Ⓓ

REGENT'S PARK

MAIDA VALE

Kensal Green Cemetery ◉

NORTH KENSINGTON

*Grand Union Canal*

WESTWAY

EDGWARE ROAD

MARYLEBONE ROAD

MARYLEBONE

Waterbus Rides to Camden ◉

PADDINGTON

Portobello Road Market ⑤

Redemption Bar ⑤

OXFORD

Core by Clare Smyth ⑤

BAYSWATER

BAYSWATER ROAD

Music and Video Exchange ⑤

NOTTING HILL

*Kensington Gardens*

*Hyde Park*

PARK LANE

MAYFAIR

HOLLAND PARK AVENUE

Serpentine Lido ◉

PICCADILLY

*Green Park*

*Holland Park*

KENSINGTON HIGH STREET

KENSINGTON ROAD

KENSINGTON

KNIGHTSBRIDGE

Science Museum ⓐ

SLOANE ST

CROMWELL ROAD

Natural History Museum ⓐ

ⓐ V&A

SOUTH KENSINGTON

WEST KENSINGTON

Saatchi Gallery ⓐ

CHELSEA

*Ranelagh Gardens*

FULHAM ROAD

KING'S ROAD

CHELSEA EMBANKMENT

*Thames*

LILLIE ROAD

Brompton Cemetery ◉

*Battersea Park*

Market Hall Fulham ⑤

FULHAM PALACE ROAD

FULHAM

The Magic Garden ⑩

BATTERSEA BRIDGE RD

BATTERSEA PARK RD

NEW KING'S ROAD

Mien Tay ⑤

BATTERSEA

Sightsee aboard the Thames Clipper ◉

YORK ROAD

The Half Moon ⑩

Walk the Thames Path ◉

PUTNEY

The Ship ⑩

0 kilometres    1

0 miles    1

MAP 4

**4**

BLOOMSBURY

STREET

SOHO

CHARING CROSS RD

St James's
Park

WESTMINSTER

VAUXHALL BRIDGE RD

Tate
Britain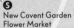

PIMLICO

GROSVENOR RD

NINE ELMS LANE

New Covent Garden
Flower Market

NINE
ELMS

## E EAT

Core by Clare Smyth *(p38)*
Market Hall Fulham *(p43)*
Mien Tay *(p53)*
Redemption Bar *(p44)*

## D DRINK

The Half Moon *(p79)*
The Magic Garden *(p69)*
The Ship *(p68)*

## S SHOP

Music and Video Exchange *(p95)*
New Covent Garden Flower
   Market *(p105)*
Portobello Road Market *(p89)*

## A ARTS & CULTURE

Natural History Museum *(p120)*
Saatchi Gallery *(p126)*
Science Museum  *(p123)*
Tate Britain *(p123)*
V&A *(p121)*

## O OUTDOORS

Brompton Cemetery *(p179)*
Kensal Green Cemetery *(p177)*
Serpentine Lido *(p164)*
Sightsee aboard the
   Thames Clipper *(p172)*
Walk the Thames Path *(p173)*
Waterbus Rides to Camden *(p175)*

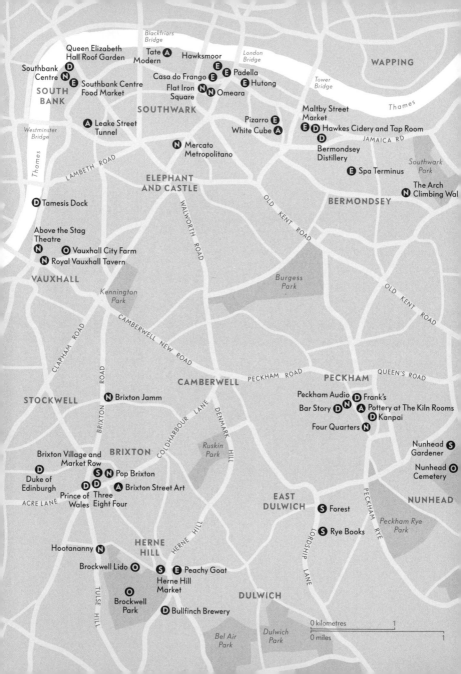

Blackfriars Bridge

London Bridge

WAPPING

Queen Elizabeth Hall Roof Garden

Tate Modern

Hawksmoor

Southbank Centre

Southbank Centre Food Market

SOUTH BANK

Casa do Frango

Flat Iron Square

Padella

Hutong

Omeara

SOUTHWARK

Tower Bridge

Thames

Maltby Street Market

Pizarro

White Cube

Hawkes Cidery and Tap Room

JAMAICA RD

Westminster Bridge

Leake Street Tunnel

Mercato Metropolitano

Bermondsey Distillery

Southwark Park

Thames

ELEPHANT AND CASTLE

BERMONDSEY

Spa Terminus

The Arch Climbing Wal

Tamesis Dock

Old Kent Road

Above the Stag Theatre

Vauxhall City Farm

Royal Vauxhall Tavern

VAUXHALL

Kennington Park

Burgess Park

OLD KENT ROAD

CAMBERWELL NEW ROAD

PECKHAM ROAD

CAMBERWELL

PECKHAM

QUEEN'S ROAD

Peckham Audio

Frank's

STOCKWELL

Brixton Jamm

Bar Story

Pottery at The Kiln Rooms

Kanpai

Four Quarters

BRIXTON ROAD

CLAPHAM ROAD

COLDHARBOUR LANE

DENMARK HILL

Ruskin Park

Nunhead Gardener

Nunhead Cemetery

Brixton Village and Market Row

Duke of Edinburgh

Pop Brixton

Brixton Street Art

BRIXTON

Prince of Wales

Three Eight Four

ACRE LANE

EAST DULWICH

NUNHEAD

Forest

Peckham Rye Park

Hootananny

Brockwell Lido

Peachy Goat

Rye Books

HERNE HILL

Herne Hill Market

LORDSHIP LANE

PECKHAM RYE

Brockwell Park

DULWICH

TULSE HILL

HERNE HILL

Bullfinch Brewery

0 kilometres          1

0 miles          1

Bel Air Park

Dulwich Park

MAP 5

**5**

Surrey Docks Farm

**N** Printworks

**ROTHERHITHE**

**N** Big Dyke Energy

**NEW CROSS**

**A** London Terrariums

**BROCKLEY**

Brockley **O** Cemetery

*Camberwell Cemetery*

MAP 6

LOUGHTON

HIGWELL

**6**

REDBRIDGE

ILFORD

BARKING

East End
Women's Museum **A**

EAST HAM

WOOLWICH

CHARLTON

**⊙** Charlton Lido

ELTHAM

CHISLEHURST

BROMLEY

FARNBOROUGH

Thames

## **E** EAT

Ariana II *(p55)*
Brockley Market *(p42)*
Greenwich Market *(p40)*
Milk *(p35)*
Petersham Nurseries *(p38)*
Punjab House *(p55)*
Xi'an Impression *(p54)*

## **D** DRINK

Crate Brewery *(p82)*
The Devonshire *(p79)*
The Gipsy Moth *(p71)*
The Prospect of Whitby *(p70)*
The Spaniards Inn *(p76)*

## **S** SHOP

Aladdin's Cave *(p88)*
Audio Gold *(p92)*
Cornercopia *(p102)*
God's Own Junkyard *(p102)*
Little Record Shop *(p92)*
New Beacon Books *(p99)*

## **A** ARTS & CULTURE

Camden Art Centre *(p127)*
East End Women's Museum *(p115)*
Fish Island *(p118)*

Museum of London
   Docklands *(p112)*
Now Gallery *(p127)*
The Old Police Station *(p126)*
Ragged School Museum *(p114)*
Social Pottery *(p129)*

## **N** NIGHTLIFE

Adonis at The Cause *(p159)*
FOLD *(p153)*
Model Market *(p137)*
Roof East *(p142)*
Tooting Market *(p139)*
Tooting Tram & Social *(p154)*
Union Chapel *(p145)*

## **O** OUTDOORS

Charlton Lido *(p165)*
Crystal Palace Park *(p171)*
Follow the Wandle Trail *(p173)*
Hampstead Heath *(p169)*
Hampstead Heath Ponds *(p166)*
Highgate Cemetery *(p176)*
Parliament Hill Lido *(p166)*
Primrose Hill *(p170)*
Richmond Park *(p168)*
Tooting Bec Lido *(p166)*
Walthamstow Wetlands *(p175)*
Wandsworth Cemetery *(p178)*

# EAT

*Food comes in many guises in London: unhurried brunches, cosy pub roasts, sociable street food feasts. Whatever the meal, it's all about good food and good company.*

# Brunch Spots

*Whether it's a jubilant affair with all the gang or a lingering feast for two, brunch is the hallmark of a proper weekend. And London is chock-full of brunch spots to lure locals away from the comfort of bed.*

## THE GOOD EGG

**Map 3; 93 Stoke Newington Church Street, Stoke Newington;**
**///friend.fuels.pram; www.thegoodegg.co**

The Good Egg's all-day breakfasts have become a queue-inducing weekend ritual for Stokey's effortlessly trendy locals. The café's calm nook of wooden tables, stripped floorboards and whitewashed walls lined with jars of pickled lemons forms a backdrop for the exchanging of stories: families pass around sweet braided babka,

### Try it!
### MAKE A BABKA

The Good Egg's chocolate babka is one of London's cult baked delights, and one slice is just not enough. Buy a bake-your-own kit to take away; it comes with all the ingredients and instructions.

grown-up friends gather over Jerusalem-inspired sharing plates, and 20-somethings toast to the hair of the dog with the jubilant clink of Prosecco glasses.

## ST JOHN BREAD & WINE

**Map 2; 94–6 Commercial Street, Shoreditch; ///exit.cover.rods; www.stjohnrestaurant.com**

Nothing says confidence like a short, simple menu. And St John's stripped-back breakfast, offering a handful of old-school classics like bacon sandwiches and grilled kippers on sourdough, is rightly confident. Maybe it's the rare-breed bacon, or the nose-to-tail philosophy – whatever it is, St John's has become a local institution and a great place to fuel up before browsing Spitalfields Market.

**>> Don't leave without** bagging your own fresh made-to-order madeleines – the perfect sweet finish to a savoury brunch.

## THE COAL OFFICE

**Map 1; 2 Bagley Walk, Coal Drops Yard, Kings Cross; ///rooms.inch.shaky www.coaloffice.com**

In-the-know Londoners were there the minute Coal Drops Yard opened, snapping away at this industrial sweep of Victorian railway arches transformed with concept stores and stylish restaurants. And they were there when The Coal Office – a meeting of minds between designer Tom Dixon and chef Assaf Granit – launched. Those first fans still haven't left; join them on the terrace for coffees and sharing plates of Middle Eastern-inspired dishes.

# MILLFIELDS COFFEE

**Map 3; 145 Chatsworth Road, Clapton; ///delay.safety.cove;**
**www.millfieldscoffee.co.uk**

Under pastel-pink signage and with an airy dining room that spills onto a generous slab of pavement opposite Millfields Park, this is a favourite spot for young couples with gurgling babies and catch-ups with friends over brews. It's a slice of low-key Clapton life, especially on Sundays thanks to the proper East End market just outside.

**» Don't leave without** trying the Turkish eggs. Steeped in oil and whipped yoghurt, they're impossibly silky and rich.

# TOWPATH CAFÉ

**Map 3; 42 De Beauvoir Crescent, Haggerston; ///erase.gears.face;**
**www.towpathcafe.wordpress.com**

The trio of food-fanatics that run this canalside caff have garnered a cult following for their cheese toasties, but hipsters keep coming back for the coffee, changing menu and cheerful, casual set-up. Settle in on the makeshift furniture and let your entertainment be the constant stream of bikes whizzing along the canal.

# CARAVAN

**Map 1; 11–13 Exmouth Market, Farringdon; ///strike.decide.sings;**
**www.caravanrestaurants.co.uk**

Billed as "well-travelled food" owing to its globally inspired sharing plates, this small London chain dishes up mouthwatering fusion fare: think deep-fried duck egg with baba ghanoush, chorizo oil and

If Caravan is full, nab a spot at nearby Berber & Q, where you'll find small plates and Middle Eastern spices. crispy shallots. Pair with a flat white from the in-house roastery and you'll be set up for exploring Exmouth Market. Grab a table on its corner-side terrace if you can.

## MILK

### Map 6; 18–20 Bedford Hill, Balham; ///melt.give.trucks; www.milklondonshop.uk

This spot at the tail end of Balham's Hildreth Market is no secret. The place to see and be seen, queuing for an hour on a Saturday to snag a tiny table is a rite of passage. It may not be as fairly priced as some of the smaller spots that line the same street, but the setting is unbeatable. Join fashionable groups of young people sipping on coffees alfresco – come rain or shine – and watch flower traders sell their blooms at the other end of the cobblestone street.

## BISTROTHEQUE

### Map 2; 23–27 Wadeson Street, Bethnal Green; ///regard.open.amuse; www.bistrotheque.com

Don't be fooled by the industrial exterior of Bistrotheque. Enveloped in an interior of greys and whites, this is where Londoners head when they want to show how grown up they are. Parents in town? In-laws visiting? A birthday brunch without the all-you-can-drink connotations? The above would all work nicely here, especially if the pianist makes an appearance. And the food – modern fusion dishes that meld unusual ingredients and British produce – is set to impress too.

# Special Occasion

*London knows how to mark an occasion. From the drama of flames dancing in open kitchens to gorgeous flower-draped settings, there's a memorable dining experience to mark birthdays, promotions and more.*

## KILN

**Map 1; 58 Brewer Street, Soho; ///stray.puppy.gains; www.kilnsoho.com**

The style at this Thai barbecue restaurant is performative – a gleaming counter runs the length of the compact space giving diners a view of the open-kitchen – but the atmosphere is casual and laid-back. Inspired by Thai roadside eateries, the food here comprises flame-licked meats, curries served in clay pots and ember-charred vegetables. Repeat customers head to the back to talk to the chefs over the soundtrack of chatter and bubbling pots.

## NOBU

**Map 2; 10–50 Willow Street, Hackney; ///arts.hired.asset;**
**www.noburestaurants.com**

Sleek concrete, seductive lighting and a back-lit bar – if you needed proof that once-gritty Shoreditch has grown up then this is it. Set in the basement of Nobu's hotel, the restaurant draws a stylish clientele

Can't get a booking at Nobu? Head to Roka, Canary Wharf, for more show-stopping Japanese fare.

who pore over delicate Japanese-Peruvian dishes – slithers of sashimi and heaps of zingy ceviche – while the gentle thrum of chatter provides a buzzing vibe.

# TEMPER

### Map 1; 25 Broadwick Street, Soho; ///length.drift.poetic; www.temperrestaurant.com

The smell of wood smoke creeps up the staircase to greet you as you arrive at this seductive barbecue restaurant. Bag a seat at the sleek counter-top, which is crammed right up close to the drama of the vast firepit, and watch the butchering of carcasses, the flash of flames and fragrant muddling of cocktails.

**»** **Don't leave without** ordering some paratha, a flaky, silky wrap that somehow brings to mind the buttery centre of a croissant.

# HAWKSMOOR

### Map 5; 16 Winchester Walk, Borough; ///spot.oiled.ties; www.thehawksmoor.com

With six branches across London, you'd fear renowned steakhouse Hawksmoor might have got a bit too big for its boots by now. But thankfully it keeps ticking all the boxes: steak sourced from small British farms, sustainable seafood and an impressive cocktail list. Tucked around the corner from the market, the Borough branch – an elegantly industrial former warehouse – is always packed on Sundays with sophisticated patrons splashing out on wallet-draining roasts.

# YAUATCHA

**Map 1; 15–17 Broadwick Street, Soho; ///famed.trucks.truly;**
**www.yauatcha.com**

Is this the best dim sum in London? It's certainly up there. Dimly lit
Yauatcha is the creation of Alan Yau, the brains behind Hakkasan,
Wagamama and Busaba Eathai. But London's foodies favour
Yauatcha. Scallop shui mai melts like butter; venison puffs crumble to
moist perfection; honey roast pork oozes from char sui buns. Yes, the
à la carte dumplings can tot up to a hefty bill, but it's definitely worth it.

# CORE BY CLARE SMYTH

**Map 4; 92 Kensington Park Road, Notting Hill; ///saying.strike.risen;**
**www.corebyclaresmyth.com**

Northern Irish Clare Smyth is the first and only female British chef to
gain three Michelin stars. Her achievements deserve a shout out,
but it's her seasonal and artful menu that's worthy of celebration.
Round off an exultant meal at the bar, where the friendly bartenders
will mix you a killer cocktail.

# PETERSHAM NURSERIES

**Map 6; Off Church Lane, Petersham Road, Richmond;**
**///smile.voices.liked; www.petershamnurseries.com**

Yes, there is a Petersham Nurseries restaurant in Covent Garden but
it just doesn't compare to the original outpost. You'd struggle to find
a more beautiful setting – tucked down a muddy lane, this oasis feels
nothing like London. Set within a garden centre, the glasshouse

restaurant transports you to the Med: a bougainvillea-draped ceiling, bowls full of lemons atop worn wooden tables and the heady scent of jasmine. It's as much about the setting as it is the menu, which is inspired by the nursery garden and what's in season. After your celebratory lunch, treat yourself to something in the shop – you deserve it.

## HUTONG

**Map 5; Level 33, The Shard, 31 St Thomas Street, London Bridge; ///villa.epic.pound; www.hutong.co.uk**

Any special occasion is made extra memorable by a spectacular view. The Shard has a number of swanky restaurants but Hutong's panoramic views, northern Chinese menu and creative cocktail list take some beating. There's also a fixed-price lunch menu, making for both an affordable and stellar meal.

## ROVI

**Map 1; 59 Wells Street, Fitzrovia; ///points.closer.purely; www.ottolenghi.co.uk**

Israeli-English chef Yotam Ottolenghi is a local icon famed for his inventive creations, and his Fitzrovia restaurant promises a truly special meal without the waiting list. The menu is led by a cast of cleverly executed vegetable dishes while meat and fish play supporting roles. When it comes to making a toast, take your time perusing the wine list, which is dedicated to organic bottles by small producers.

**» Don't leave without** tucking into the celeriac shawarma, especially if you're a meat-eater – you'll forget this kebab is veggie.

# Street Food

*On a budget? Some of the best food in London is dished up from food trucks and makeshift stalls. Try everything: you might be sampling the work of the city's next big chef.*

## GREENWICH MARKET

**Map 6; 5B Greenwich Market, Greenwich; ///darker.forum.doors; www.greenwichmarket.london**

They say half the fun is getting there – arrive in Greenwich by boat and you've certainly started things off right. Follow your nose, and the locals, to its historical covered market, held Thursday through to Sunday. Surrounded by independents, the street food stalls offer a wealth of options: the fragrantly spiced pomegranate-speckled wraps, gooey brownies and flaky empanadas all have a loyal following.

## MALTBY STREET MARKET

**Map 5; Ropewalk, Bermondsey; ///grabs.fled.actors; www.maltby.st**

Forget the hubbub of Borough Market. Come the weekend and London's foodies have one place in mind – Maltby Street Market. Bermondsey's Ropewalk, a narrow passage between Victorian railway arches strung with festoon lights and fluttering flags, makes

Maltby Street Market is the perfect place to fuel up before tackling Bermondsey's beloved Beer Mile. an attractive backdrop. Run the gourmet gauntlet between traders, or duck into the railway arches to discover *jamón* shops and small-batch gin bars.

## SOUTHBANK CENTRE FOOD MARKET

### Map 5; Belvedere Road, South Bank; ///rift.stews.dips;
### www.southbankcentre.co.uk

A trip to the South Bank is an absolute must for any visitor to London – it's hard to beat the cultural centre's city vistas and the lively atmosphere along the riverside walkway. Time your arrival for a late lunch at this small but perfectly formed weekend food market, tucked just behind the Royal Festival Hall. Some of London's most diverse dishes can be sampled here, and there's always time for a freshly poured ale, best enjoyed on a Thameside bench looking onto the Houses of Parliament and the London Eye.

» **Don't leave without** trying one of The Frenchie's famous duck confit burgers with melted cheese and duck fat-fried chips.

### Try it!
### JOIN A BAKING CLASS

Near Maltby Street you'll find busy Borough Market and baking school Bread Ahead (*www.breadahead.com*). Join a half-day course and learn how to make buttery croissants or oil-rich focaccia bread.

## SPA TERMINUS

**Map 5; Dockley Road Industrial Estate, Bermondsey;**
**///spins.wooden.minute; www.spa-terminus.co.uk**

Spa Terminus is the place locals really don't want to share. Here the railway arches are home to the headquarters of some of the city's best independent food businesses, which on Saturdays open to the public. Join sets of 30-something friends as they peruse the organic vegetables, biodynamic wines and artisan cheeses – all while clutching invigorating cups of Monmouth coffee.

## BROCKLEY MARKET

**Map 6; Lewisham College car park, Brockley; ///paying.loans.entire;**
**www.brockleymarket.com**

Every Saturday a humble car park is transformed into one of London's best farmers' markets. Fresh produce abounds – mounds of organic fruit and veg, stacks of cheese and glistening fish. Young couples flock here, alongside families with pushchairs and dogs looking longingly at the butcher's counter. Browse the stalls, sampling as you go, but leave space for lunch from one of the street food trucks.

## SEVEN DIALS MARKET

**Map 1; 35 Earlham Street, Covent Garden; ///mess.army.flip;**
**www.sevendialsmarket.com**

This centrally located spot is often overlooked by visitors, but Londoners in the know love this indoor food hall, which is open Friday through Monday. Here you'll discover a tempting variety of food outlets at street level, serving a diverse selection of food and cocktails. Head downstairs to eat at communal tables with professionals breaking for lunch or gaggles of friends welcoming the weekend with rounds of beers.

# EXMOUTH MARKET

**Map 1; Exmouth Market, Clerkenwell; ///prep.empty.teach;**
**www.exmouth.london**

Come lunchtime, make a beeline for this pedestrianized street of food stalls, open every Monday through Saturday. There are just a dozen stands, so be sure you get there sooner rather than later – it's so popular that local workers will have snapped up most of the food by 2pm. Hang around the area until the evening, when it's time for after-work beers and table football at Café Kick.

**» Don't leave without** trying a steaming bowl of Ghanaian lamb stew, fried plantain and tomato-rich jollof rice from Spinach & Agushi.

# MARKET HALL FULHAM

**Map 4; 472 Fulham Road, Fulham; ///posed.rated.really;**
**www.markethalls.co.uk**

Tube stations and great food rarely go hand in hand but Fulham's Market Hall bucks this trend. Housed in an ornate Edwardian entrance hall that once served the Tube, this buzzing food market has become a local foodie favourite. Pencil pushers nip here for lunchtime kebabs, freelancers sip flat whites and tap away at laptops, and crowds arrive at night for plump fried chicken and drinks on the roof.

# Plant-Based

*London was named the vegan capital of the world in 2019. And with 150 vegan restaurants – including our favourites listed here – even meat-eaters will be tempted by the plant-based revolution.*

## REDEMPTION BAR

**Map 4; 6 Chepstow Road, Notting Hill; ///liver.people.pounds;**
**www.redemptionbar.co.uk**

Any meal taken at Redemption comes with a healthy side portion of smugness: nothing on the menu is bad for you, or for the planet. The dining room's all white walls and low-hanging lamps, while the menu is 100 per cent vegan, sugar-free, wheat-free and booze-free. "Spoil yourself without spoiling yourself", the entrepreneurial owners say – and who can argue when the miso aubergine is this good?

## ANDU CAFÉ

**Map 3; 528 Kingsland Road, Dalston; ///risen.clip.pouch;**
**www.anducafe.com**

Ethiopian cuisine might just be the world's most vegan-friendly, with spicy beans, pulses and greens in oil-rich curries. This cash-only canteen has been serving it up since 1970 – long before the vegan trend hit Dalston. It's BYO, only charges £7 a head (takeaway spreads for a fiver) and feels like you're eating in a neighbour's living room. If you're looking to be introduced to injera – a traditional spongy, fermented pancake – look no further.

## THE SPREAD EAGLE

**Map 3; 224 Homerton High Street, Hackney; ///glee.bonus.locate; www.thespreadeaglelondon.co.uk**

London's first 100 per cent vegan pub was savvy enough to throw open its cruelty-free doors in Veganuary 2018, creating serious hype over its animal product-free beers. Today the coquettishly named Spread Eagle prides itself on its minimal-waste kitchen and pub grub made from locally produced and foraged ingredients. Even meat-eating hipsters keep returning to this forward-thinking gastropub for another slap-up meal.

**» Don't leave without** trying the ploughman's lunch, complete with a porkless pie. It's great medicine on a drizzly day.

## PEACHY GOAT

**Map 5; 16 Half Moon Lane, Herne Hill; ///spend.wished.gross; www.peachygoat.com**

Vegan versions of all the bistro classics you can imagine come together at this adorable café run by three childhood friends. The eco-conscious menu uses 100 per cent natural ingredients to make a range of hearty plates – from a mouthwatering "sausage" sandwich to a filling "blue cheese" burger to a decadent sticky toffee pudding.

## UNITY DINER

**Map 2; 60 Wentworth Street, Spitalfields; ///bonus.wiring.myself;**
**www.unitydiner.co.uk**

Designed for vegans and flexitarians, this 100-seat, non-profit,
earth-friendly diner – run by vegan activist Earthling Ed – is as
much a centre for public education around mass food production
and animal cruelty as it is a place to sink your teeth into a soy
Chikken burger with melted Cheeze.

## BLACK CAT CAFÉ

**Map 3; 76A Clarence Road, Hackney; ///intervals.cotton.rabble;**
**www.blackcatcafe.co.uk**

You know you're onto a local secret when a restaurant with plain décor
and a few wooden benches is packed to the rafters. As well as epic
brunches, this independent workers' cooperative sells locally made
products and has a bookshop stocked with plant-based cookbooks.
**» Don't leave without** trying a homemade vegan sausage roll, which
varies in shape and size according to the batch of the day.

## RUDY'S VEGAN DINER

**Map 1; 729–731, Camden Stables Market, Camden;**
**///single.crop.wisdom; www.rudysvegan.com**

You don't need to feel guilty about chowing down on a "dirty" burger at
Rudy's Vegan Diner, where soya mince patties are topped with cashew
cheese, fake bacon and all the salady accoutrements. Wash down
with a milk-free shake for the ultimate not-so-greasy spoon experience.

## Liked by the locals

"What's unique about London is its huge variety, accessibility and density of vegan restaurants. You can get vegan fried chicken, cheesy stuffed crust pizza, healthy vegan food if you want to – and it's all happened in the past five years. It makes me excited to think where we'll be five years from now."

ED WINTER, UNITY DINER FOUNDER

# Comfort Food

*This is a city that loves to indulge, whether that's with silky noodles wrapped in butter, oozing cheese toasties or burgers sandwiched between glazed brioche buns. Now's not the time to hold back.*

## CHEESE BAR

### Map 1; Unit 93–4 Camden Stables, Camden Town;
### ///rival.rivers.just; www.thecheesebar.com

The Cheese Bar has elevated melted cheese – that wonderful gooey pick-me-up – to higher ranks with this little nook of a restaurant decked out in industrial chic. Cheese fiends, get your fix here. Gobble handfuls of mozzarella sticks on the sun-dappled terrace or a bubbling pan of mac 'n' cheese at the bar.

## PADELLA

### Map 5; 6 Southwark Street, London Bridge; ///best.storm.little;
### www.padella.co

Pillowy ravioli, silken pappardelle, nostalgic nests of spaghetti – few comfort foods beat the carby embrace of pasta. And Padella brings an added layer of comfort to the dish, that of predictability: you can tell the time with one glance at this restaurant. Mornings are a lull of calm,

Cheat Padella's queue by downloading Clever Queue. As long as you're nearby, the app will queue for you, so you can enjoy a drink.

the windows framing the ritual of rolling pasta; come mid-morning a queue of office workers signals the hope of lunch; by evening the queue reappears, and inside thrums with chatter.

# G KELLY

**Map 2; 526 Roman Road, Bow; ///newly.comb.tells; www.gkelly.london**

Long wanted to taste the classic East End dish, jellied eels? Of course you have. And at G Kelly – where they've been rustling up that dish since 1939 – you're in safe hands. This is one of East London's last-remaining traditional pie and mash shops, a family business that closed only for a two-year refurb in 2017. Minced beef pie, with mash, parsley sauce "liquor" and eels, is especially popular with Cockney locals. There's even a vegan pie on the menu now, too.

# CASA DO FRANGO

**Map 5; 32 Southwark Street, London Bridge; ///pure.thin.aspect; www.casadofrango.co.uk**

Forget Nando's, Casa do Frango will cure even the most devilish of grilled chicken cravings. Of course, charcoal-grilled piri piri is the main event here, but the authentic Portuguese flavours infuse a series of moreish extras: crispy chicken-skin-flecked African rice, fizzing goblets of Port Tonic, oozy *pasteis de nata*. And the space is gorgeous too.

**» Don't leave without** visiting the hidden bar. Smuggled away behind a velvet curtain, this brooding setting is perfect date territory.

# Solo, Pair, Crowd

**Whether you're grabbing a bite to eat on your own or feasting en masse, there's a foodie spot for you.**

### SOLO

**Comfort food with a book**

Some meals are best shared with a good book. Cosy up with your current read at the E Pellicci in Bethnal Green. The Italian greasy spoon dishes up stellar fry-ups and strong builder's tea.

### IN A PAIR

**Wallet-friendly catch-ups**

Known for seasonal Italian food in a cool industrial space, Peckham's Forza Wine serves up pasta and a glass of wine for a tenner nightly between 6 and 7pm.

### IN A CROWD

**Competitive Sunday roasts**

The Alma Pub in Newington Green is known for three things: first-rate roasts (you'll need to book ahead), its Sunday evening pub quizzes and the quirky movie memorabilia that dots its interior.

# BAO

**Map 1; 53 Lexington Street, Soho; ///decks.drift.clown; www.baolondon.com**

Everything about this place is little (apart from the rather infamous queue to get in, that is): the tiny, pared-back interior; the short paper menu you scribble your selections on; the bite-sized steamed milk buns that have given their namesake restaurant this cult following. Diminutive yes, but this isn't dainty dining – expect to leave over-stuffed on bites of tender pork-confit bao and crispy fried chicken.

# LUCKY CHIP

**Map 2; 44 Essex Road, Angel; ///cups.stuck.driver;
www.theoldqueenshead.com**

The gourmet burger residency at beloved Angel pub The Old Queen's Head has garnered a gang of regulars for its just-greasy-enough patties and simple toppings. The pub hosts some of the best hip hop nights in north London so be sure to stick around for the evening.

**» Don't leave without** trying El Chappo, an epic spice-fest of roasted jalapeños and bacon layered on a blue-cheese-laden beef patty.

# LAHORE KEBAB HOUSE

**Map 2; 2–10 Umberston Street, Whitechapel; ///social.beats.outfit;
www.lahore-kebabhouse.com**

London wouldn't be London without its curry houses, and Pakistani-owned Lahore promises a truly comforting slap-up meal. Don't be fooled by this local icon's modest appearance; you'll find queues of hopefuls, all clutching bags of booze (it's BYO), here on weekends.

# Global Grub

*London's glorious diversity is echoed in its food scene.
Get to know the city's locals over a hearty meal –
whether you're chowing down in a Vietnamese
stalwart or a family-run Indian kitchen.*

## GUNPOWDER

### Map 2; 11 White's Row, Spitalfields; ///email.sheets.adding;
### www.gunpowderlondon.com

A mother-and-son team runs this tiny Indian restaurant in Spitalfields,
where bare-brick walls reflect the blend of chic and homemade on
the menu. The sophisticated small plates include Kashmiri lamb
chops and a whole broccoli head doused in yoghurt and spices.
If you're the type to test your mettle on a vindaloo, wash it all down
with a chilli-spiked mimosa, which gets spicier as you drink.

## THE BARBARY

### Map 1; 16 Neal's Yard, Covent Garden; ///couple.forced.critic;
### www.thebarbary.co.uk

If you have to queue anywhere then Neal's Yard is best – a
colour-splashed, plant-strewn nook of a courtyard that's ideal for
people-watching. Once you're seated inside The Barbary, the

visual stimulation continues; an eclectic crowd eats at the 24-seat counter bar encircling the drama of the open kitchen. And the food, an almost indecipherable list of ingredients set to transport you to North Africa, is second to none.

# PIZARRO

**Map 5; 104 Bermondsey Street, Bermondsey; ///fails.free.tasty; www.josepizarro.com**

Spanish chef José Pizarro has taken on Bermondsey as his own, which is lucky for foodies who get to step into a corner of Spain when they book dinner at this spot. Chef Pizarro takes the freshest, highest-quality ingredients and proves he's the master of traditional Iberian cooking with staples such as slow-braised beef stew.

**» Don't leave without** kicking things off with the acorn-fed jamón Ibérico. Be warned: it is expensive, but it's worth every penny.

# MIEN TAY

**Map 4; 122 Kingsland Road, Hackney; ///option.care.poet; www. mientay.co.uk**

Just one taste of the butter-soft galangal goat curry makes it clear why this spot has a loyal fan base among its Hackney locals. The Kingsland Road branch of this authentic, southwest Vietnamese kitchen is a legend of "pho mile" – the stretch of Vietnamese restaurants between Shoreditch and Hoxton. Since it became famous for its fragrant phos and clay pot curries, the family-run restaurant has opened three other branches, all headed up by a different family member.

# XI'AN IMPRESSION

**Map 6; 117 Benwell Road, Arsenal; ///summer.glove.punk;
www.xianimpression.co.uk**

This teeny-tiny, BYO, strip-lit canteen almost didn't make it into
this book – it's a neighbourhood secret that's too good to share.
But we've decided to let you in on it. Here, chef Wei Guirong serves
authentic street food from the Shan Xi province of China, home
to the Terracotta Warriors. And, oh boy, is she talented. The menu
is all hand-pulled noodles, pot sticker dumplings and wonderfully
gloopy pulled-pork "burgers" – far more akin to a bready bao than
an American-style bun. Comforting, bold-flavoured and dripping
in juices, the food at Xi'an Impression might just change your life.
But be a pal and keep it to yourself, eh?

» **Don't leave without** trying the signature starter: a chilled bowl of
hand-pulled noodles, stirred through with cucumber matchsticks and
wonderfully spongy tofu.

**Shh!**

Londoners have an obsession
with supper clubs. They love
nothing more than an exclusive,
small-time dining experience,
where seasonal, inventive grub
meets interesting company and
sultry vibes. All three abound
at Peckham's Kanpai *(p80)*,

London's only sake brewery. Run
by a craft-brewing power couple,
the taproom also hosts seasonal
dinners with Japanese flair:
think raw sea bass cured with
citrus, or smoked ribs and ginger
rice, all paired with a range of
sakes. Booking is essential.

## ARIANA II

**Map 6; 241 Kilburn High Street, Kilburn; ///path.sings.part;**
**www.ariana2.uk**

This family-run Afghan restaurant started across the pond in Manhattan. Back here in West London, Ariana II dishes out warm welcomes and meat kebabs in homely surrounds. It's BYO, making the whole evening extra affordable, but forgo the booze and wash it all down with the delicious mint-yogurt dough drink instead.

## PUNJAB HOUSE

**Map 6; 37 Balham High Road, Balham; ///blog.tile.zeal;**
**www.punjabhouse.co.uk**

This is the kind of restaurant that everyone wants at the end of their road. Family-run Punjab House has been thrilling South Londoners since 1985 with its hearty Punjabi home cooking. Groups of friends pile in on Saturdays and Sundays to tuck into the Nihari weekend special (slow-cooked spicy lamb shank that melts in the mouth) and chat to endlessly smiley head honcho Shazia.

## FLORAL BY LIMA

**Map 1; 14 Garrick Street, Covent Garden; ///feels.shield.soccer;**
**www.limalondongroup.com**

Forget Michelin-star winner Floral. Sister restaurant Floral by LIMA plates up equally delicious Peruvian food and, better still, without the hefty price tag. It's a great choice for date night; tuck into ceviche and empanadas before a nightcap downstairs in the low-lit Alpaca Bar.

### Feed your sweet tooth at
## AMBALA

Queues snake out the door of this Pakistani sweet shop during religious festivals. Treat yourself to *habshi halwa*, a fudgy cardamom-infused cake made of cashews, pistachios and almonds.

### Stock up at
## BHAVINS FOOD

Begin at one of Tooting's oldest grocery stores and stock up on spices to add to your collection.

### Lunch at
## MIRCH MASALA

Tuck into succulent slow-cooked lamb at this Indian-Pakistani institution, which is a favourite of local politician Sadiq Khan.

*Just off the main road – which locals call "land of the curry mile" – is* **Harrington's**, *which has been serving pie and mash since 1908.*

### Raise a glass at
## TOOTING MARKET

Walk off your lunch by browsing Tooting Market, which has been keeping residents' fridges stocked since 1930. Fresh produce aside – and if you still have room – there are lots of street food options here.

UPPER TOOTING

BROADWATER

ROAD

LETCHWORTH STREET

UPPER TOOTING ROAD

SELKIRK

ROAD

BLAKENHAM ROAD

STREET

TOOTING HIGH

TOTTERDOWN STREET

TOOTING BROADWAY

0 metres 100
0 yards 100

## An afternoon
# dining in Tooting

Travel south and you'll find one of London's most vibrant neighbourhoods. Trendy new restaurants are constantly popping up around Tooting Broadway, adding to a buzzing food culture that's embedded in community spirit. Tooting High Street, which stretches between Tube stops Tooting Bec and Tooting Broadway, bustles with independent, Indian and Pakistani shops that reflect the multicultural demographics of the area. Come Eid or Diwali, there's no more exciting place to be, sampling locally made sweets and revelling in the celebratory atmosphere.

**1. Bhavins Food**
193–7 Upper
Tooting Road;
///sums.supporter.search

**2. Ambala**
201 Upper Tooting Road;
www.ambalafoods.com;
///soda.rope.sooner

**3. Mirch Masala**
213 Upper Tooting Road;
www.mirchmasala-takeaway.co.uk
///tried.view.richer

**4. Tooting Market**
21–23 Tooting High Street;
www.tootingmarket.com
///shells.labs.straw

**Harrington's** ///flood.angle.scope

# DRINK

*Pubs and cafés are the beating heart of London's social scene. Days pass catching up in cute indie coffee shops, and nights are spent bantering in buzzing beer gardens.*

# Coffee Shops

*London's coffee scene is thriving, with independent cafés mushrooming across the city, from artisan coffee shops showcasing their locally roasted brews to coffee bars plonked in the most unexpected places.*

## DARK ARTS COFFEE

### Map 3; Arch 216, 27A Ponsford Street, Homerton; ///woes.canny.mile; www.darkartscoffee.co.uk

Tattoos, beards, a sign declaring "I will kill again" – if you thought the dark arts were just found in *Harry Potter*, think again. This place has a rebellious streak – heavy metal plays, horror film ads line the walls and the owners will happily tell you they've never made a business decision sober. Take it in while sipping your coffee in the roastery.

## POPHAMS

### Map 3; 197 Richmond Road, Hackney; ///gosh.prices.slips; www.pophamsbakery.com

If you like your coffee with a little something to nibble on, then pop over to Pophams. Sacks of flour packed high along the walls announce the bakery – here you can enjoy your cappuccino while watching the artisan bakers craft delicious mango custard Danishes.

# PALM VAULTS

**Map 3; 411 Mare Street, Hackney; ///daily.chains.rapid;**
**www.palmvaults.com**

Tribes of girlfriends armed with their phones descend in their masses upon pretty Palm Vaults to snap away at its pink walls and hanging plants. That's before they turn to the menu, which specializes in the most colourful coffees in all of London (think lavender and glitter lattes).

**» Don't leave without** trying the futuristic vegan breakfasts. Where else can you get avocado on toast with "bacon" made from coconut?

# PANGEA CAFÉ

**Map 2; 74 Commercial Street, Spitalfields; ///award.ever.mull;**
**www.pangeacafé.com**

Pangea is known colloquially as the "café in the suit shop" because, well, it's found in a suit shop. The brainchild of a forward-thinking 20-something Aussie, it's all about sustainability – from the beans through to the cups. There's even bags of compost up for grabs.

# MONMOUTH COFFEE

**Map 1; 27 Monmouth Street, Covent Garden; ///camp.normal.play;**
**www.monmouthcoffee.co.uk**

Every caffeine-addicted Londoner knows Monmouth. Having started in the basement here in 1978, the roastery has become a household name, with other branches littered across the city. But weary office workers keep returning to the tiny original for perfectly brewed coffee and small talk with the expert baristas.

## Liked by the locals

"The last decade has been an exciting one for London's speciality coffee. The bar for what constitutes great coffee is now so much higher here, meaning you can stumble upon exceptional coffee in all sorts of unexpected places."

RICHARD FRAZIER,
CHIEF MARKETING OFFICER AT WORKSHOP COFFEE

# WORKSHOP COFFEE

**Map 1; 1 Barrett Street, Marylebone; ///suffice.drew.exile;**
**www.workshopcoffee.com**

Some places just know how to do coffee right. Workshop's beans are seasonally sourced in Africa and South America and roasted in East London before they're brought here to this quiet nook in Marylebone. Perfect for those wanting a moment of zen with their caffeine.

# ALLPRESS ESPRESSO ROASTERY & CAFE

**Map 3; 55 Dalston Lane, Dalston; ///paint.badge.elder;**
**www.uk.allpressespresso.com**

Watch a batch of Allpress beans complete the careful roasting process in this joiners' factory-turned-roastery while you sip on a delicious finished brew in the café area. Sun shining? Pair a flat white with a newspaper in the leafy garden.

# OMOTESANDO KOFFEE

**Map 1; 8 Newman Street, Fitzrovia; ///fish.narrow.crisis;**
**www.ooo-koffee.com**

Having started as a little-known one-man band in a rundown tatami house in Tokyo, Omotesando now has a loyal tribe of chic devotees. This is partly down to the uber-cool minimalism, partly down to the creative coffees and partly down to the baristas who treat customers like they've known them for years.

**»  Don't leave without** trying the kashi. These baked little custard treats are like a cute cuboid take on French cannelés.

# Cocktail Joints

*London's thirst for carefully crafted cocktails – and now mocktails – seems to be unquenchable. Handily, the city is peppered with tempting cocktail bars to suit every taste, occasion and budget.*

## BAR STORY

**Map 5; 213 Blenheim Grove, Peckham; ///onions.cone.payer; www.barstory.co.uk**

With a railway arch interior slapped with white paint and dotted with candles, and an outdoor area jazzed up with a drape of festoon lights, Bar Story has perfected the effortlessly cool look. And this buzzy bar is loved by an army of London's coolest, all of whom know that the cocktails are cheap (£6 a pop, even before Happy Hour) and the thin-crusted pizzas are perfect to stave off the munchies.

## FREUD

**Map 1; 198 Shaftesbury Avenue, Covent Garden; ///thinks.alert.flats; www.freud.eu**

Tucked below street level on hectic Shaftesbury Avenue, this refreshingly unpretentious bar is a favourite of those in the know. A far cry from the glitz of its surrounding area, Freud's has a faded industrial feel – its bare concrete walls forming a blank canvas for a charged atmosphere, affordable cocktails and a rotating gallery of artworks. It's an intimate nook, the kind of place to bring a good friend or impress a date.

**»  Don't leave without** trying a gently egg-white-frothed, zesty-sweet Snow Queen cocktail – light and refreshing.

## 69 COLEBROOKE ROW

**Map 2; 69 Colebrooke Row, Islington;  ///people.stage.tamed;
www.69colebrookerow.com**

No one agrees on the name for this tiny, secretive bar. It's styled itself as "The Bar With No Name" but, given the lack of signage, for years people have simply called it 69 Colebrooke Row. What locals do agree on, though, is how good it is. Dimly lit and decked out with mid-century furnishings, this intimate bar hums with intellectual chatter as a sophisticated crowd sips on carefully crafted cocktails.

While beloved boozer The Exmouth Arms is fit to bust every weekend night, no one seems to have cottoned on to the fact that there's a secret cocktail bar right upstairs; it's so secret that it doesn't even have a website. Climb the pub's narrow staircase up to 5CC, a candlelit bar littered with inviting leather seats. Espresso martinis are elegantly made by chirpy staff for friends toasting smugly to their choice of bar.

# SPIRITLAND

**Map 1; 9–10 Stable Street, Kings Cross; ///trial.punks.posed;**
**www.spiritland.com**

This dimly lit wine and cocktail bar is a music lover's heaven, its
world-class sound system and mixing decks standing centre stage.
The music's a bit too loud for a casual chat, but most people are
here anyway to revel in the electronic sounds of DJs that would
normally sell out much bigger stages. Listen to the addictive beats
and absorb the intimate vibe while sipping on a deftly mixed cold
brew negroni or refreshing pisco punch.

# THREE EIGHT FOUR

**Map 5; 384 Coldharbour Lane, Brixton; ///venues.fear.soft;**
**www.threeeightfour.com**

This is classic date territory: exposed plasterboard and brick walls,
dim caged lighting and the atmospheric buzz of spirited chatter
filling the intimate space. You'll probably need to book to get you
and your plus one past the metal-grilled stable doors – it's a

## Try it!
## MIX YOUR OWN DRINKS

London Cocktail Club (www.london
cocktailclub.co.uk) is known for daring,
playful cocktails. Learn from the maestros
at a cocktail-making masterclass, where
you'll craft three drinks in a session.

seriously popular spot – but once you're in you can drink your way around the experimental cocktail list and unusual selection of wines and beers. Thankfully there are also small plates to soak up the booze.

# REDEMPTION BAR

### Map 1; 2 Neal's Yard, Covent Garden; ///took.shelf.gangs; www.redemptionbar.co.uk

A white-washed interior, clusters of girlfriends laughing over booze-free cocktails and friendly staff graced with a post-yoga glow – Redemption is far from your average London bar. And why shouldn't you feel clear-headed after a night of socializing? The cocktails here may largely be free of alcohol, dairy and sugar, but they taste indulgent, zinging with citrus notes and fresh botanicals.

**» Don't leave without** trying the Apple Mockjito, a refreshing blend of muddled apple, fresh mint and lime topped up with kombucha.

# UNTITLED

### Map 3; 538 Kingsland Road, Dalston; ///activism.pass.spine; www.untitled-bar.com

Rockstar mixologist Tony Conigliaro is the man to thank for the menu at this uber-creative spot, which is modelled on Andy Warhol's Silver Factory in New York. Okay, this Dalston copycat is verging on pretentious – the sparse décor is fifty shades of polished-concrete grey, with tin foil-plastered walls. But the cocktails themselves are works of alchemy. Take the Sicily – the blend of citrus, orange blossom and verbena will transport you to Italy in one sip. *Bellissimo*!

# Beer Gardens

*Few things beat the atmosphere of a London beer garden in the summer. Given even just a glimmer of sunshine and the city's pub patios – from riverside terraces to vast and buzzing yards – come alive.*

## DUKE OF EDINBURGH
### Map 5; 204 Ferndale Road, Brixton; ///smiles.exit.rift;
### www.dukeofedinburghpub.com

Tucked away from the chaos of central Brixton, the Duke of Edinburgh's vast beer garden is a welcome oasis. It's a chilled spot that, despite its size, always gets packed. Trains rumble past as groups stake their claim on the large communal tables, ready for a long afternoon of chat fuelled by local beers. When hunger strikes, the White Men Can't Jerk street food hut is handily right next to the outdoor bar.

## THE SHIP
### Map 4; 41 Jews Road, Wandsworth; ///warns.picked.title; www.theship.co.uk

For southwest Londoners, sunny weekends in the city mean one thing: long, boozy days in The Ship's beer garden. Despite being rather oddly slapped in a heavily industrial part of Wandsworth, The Ship's been a go-to since 1786. It's all about the outdoors here:

a big beer garden on the banks of the Thames, lined with long communal tables. Sports fans, rejoice: there's also a handful of heated booths each with their own TV.

**>> Don't leave without** ordering a pint of locally brewed Wandle ale, which is named after the nearby River Wandle.

# THE MAGIC GARDEN

**Map 4; 231 Battersea Park Road, Battersea; ///dates.grit.tulip; www.magicgardenpub.com**

Festival-goers feel right at home in this Battersea boozer. Its back garden is full of quirky bohemian opulence: painted vines creep along its walls, fairy lights drape overhead and a tented roof creates an indoor-outdoor tipi area dotted with sunken sofas and vintage armchairs. The Magic Garden is well known for hosting live music and its stage even transforms into a banging dance floor as the night goes on. Who needs Glasto, really?

# THE WHITE HART

**Map 3; 69 Stoke Newington High Street, Stoke Newington; ///purely.value.slice; www.whitehart stokenewington.com**

You'd never know that this imposing townhouse pub has the area's biggest secret garden out back. Make your way through the football-watching crowds clamouring at the bar and out the back to a huge green space dotted with picnic benches and strung with fairy lights. It's a down-to-earth beer garden that's not quite succumbed to the area's gentrification. If you're peckish, the pub grub is pretty solid, too.

## THE PROSPECT OF WHITBY

**Map 6; 57 Wapping Wall, Wapping; ///blocks.rooms.video;**
**www.greeneking-pubs.co.uk**

A swaying willow tree, the lapping waters of the Thames, centuries'
old charm; it's little wonder this Wapping beer garden is a favourite.
The flagstone floors of London's oldest riverside pub have borne
witness to everyone from pirates and sailors to East End criminals —
there's even a hangman's noose dangling ominously outside. Today,
the drinking den channels an altogether more welcoming vibe...

## THE ALBION

**Map 1; 10 Thornhill Road, Barnsbury; ///jazz.late.chew;**
**www.the-albion.co.uk**

Once upon a time, this flower-fronted gastropub was the watering
hole of farmers and Londoners escaping the city to rural Islington.
Today, the polluted thoroughfare of Upper Street is just down the

Shh!

Few know Hampstead's
Bohemia House *(www.
bohemiahouse.london)* so its
leafy beer garden remains a
well-kept secret. The clubhouse
was used by Czech and Slovak
immigrants after World War II,
many of whom had fought
alongside the Allied Forces.
Order a pint of Czech beer
at the bar, where the barman
will tell you more of the club's
history, before enjoying your
drink outside on the grass.

road, but you can still get a taste of the country in the pub's tree-filled, wisteria-adorned back garden. City life feels a million miles away as you sip on a draught beer and bask in the sunshine.

## PEOPLE'S PARK TAVERN

**Map 3; 360 Victoria Park Road, Hackney; ///envy.scope.monks; www. peoplesparktavern.pub**

Sprawling Victoria Park was created in 1845 for the ordinary people of the East End, earning it the moniker the People's Park. And this park-side tavern was given its name for the same reason. Beloved in the neighbourhood, it's the kind of place that caters to your every whim, whether that's a slap-up Sunday roast, a weeknight quiz or simply a kick-ass G&T to be sipped in the hacienda-style beer garden – one of London's largest, dotted with pastel-painted huts.

**» Don't leave without** trying the Mangolicious pale ale courtesy of the pub's microbrewery, the Brew Lab.

## THE GIPSY MOTH

**Map 6; 60 Greenwich Church Street, Greenwich; ///deaf.keen.snacks; www.thegipsymothgreenwich.co.uk**

Few beer gardens are watched over by a 19th-century tea clipper. Having crossed the river by the Greenwich Foot Tunnel or disembarked from one of the DLR stops, you'll find the Gipsy Moth pub is right there to welcome you. You can't miss it: it's right beside the *Cutty Sark*. Join jolly day-trippers and Greenwich residents sharing bottles of wine while you take in the ship in all its majestic glory.

# Rooftop Bars

*London's rooftops range from slick skyscraper spots to grungy converted car parks. We love them all, and the way that each area's personality shines through to a sunset backdrop of iconic views.*

## QUEEN OF HOXTON

### Map 2; 1–5 Curtain Road, Shoreditch; ///forest.tender.fade; www.queenofhoxton.com

The Queen of Hoxton is a local favourite, thanks to its wild party nights, and the rooftop is its crowning glory. It's redecorated with a new theme every season, from a 1900s Parisian salon to a candy-coloured *Wizard of Oz* world. Come winter, a huge wigwam keeps punters warm while they enjoy mulled cocktails and skyline views.

## FRANK'S

### Map 5; 10th floor, multistorey car park, 95a Rye Lane, Peckham; ///thinks.overnight.lined; www.boldtendencies.com

Peckham's worst-kept secret, Frank's rooftop bar is a local icon. Atop a multistorey car park, Frank's opens to a mixed crowd of edgy locals and edgier art students each summer. There are installations to check out (the bar is part of a local not-for-profit arts organization),

If Frank's is busy, head to the rival rooftop bar atop the Bussey Building. You'll find the Rooftop Film Club here, too.

cocktails to toast with and small plates to chow down on. The real draw, however, is the views: Londoners spend many an evening here, lingering over an Aperol Spritz as the sun sets.

## DALSTON ROOF PARK

**Map 3; 18–22 Ashwin Street, Dalston;///chair.stuck.silly; www.bootstrapcharity.com**

Only those truly in the know find their way, down an alleyway and up a flight of steps, to Dalston's only rooftop bar – an astroturfed suntrap, dotted with cocktail drinkers lounging on bean bags. It's worth the small entry fee as all profits go to investing in young people and businesses, thanks to a partnership with Bootstrap Charity. Inquire about sunrise yoga sessions and pop-up food trader residencies.

**» Don't leave without** checking out the rotating, socially minded exhibition gallery, downstairs in the Print House Gallery.

## BIG CHILL HOUSE

**Map 1; 257–9 Pentonville Road, Kings Cross; ///cape.sadly.trim; www.bigchillbar.com**

You could drink many a pint in this huge and rambling townhouse, famed for its DJ nights, without stumbling upon its roof terrace. Join the few who know about it and buy a beer from the beach shack vending station before sunning yourself in the reclining chairs. You'll feel like you're in more tropical climes, not frantic central London.

# NETIL360

## Map 3; 1 Westgate Street, London Fields; ///action.claps.jacket; www.netil360.com

It's hard to believe this place is anything more than a multistorey car park as you climb up its seemingly endless concrete stairs. But step breathlessly onto the rooftop and you'll see why Netil360 is such a hit with the cool kids. You can see far and wide – from the Shard to the Gherkin to Canary Wharf – and the complete absence of seats means you and your party can sprawl across the astroturf.

# QUEEN ELIZABETH HALL ROOF GARDEN

## Map 5; Queen Elizabeth Hall, South Bank; ///prompting.notice.reader; www.southbankcentre.co.uk

When the sun shines there's only one place London's office workers head to: the South Bank. And where do they catch the last of the sun's rays? The hidden roof garden. Climb the sunshine-yellow staircase to this oasis and sprawl amid the wildflowers and vegetable plots.

**>> Don't leave without** donating online. The roof garden is tended to by a group of volunteers who have experienced addiction, homelessness or mental health problems.

# TAMESIS DOCK

## Map 5; Albert Embankment, Lambeth; ///rods.lion.traps; www.tdock.co.uk

Okay, this bar is technically on the rooftop of a barge rather than a building, but it's too good to miss. Moored between Lambeth and Vauxhall bridges, the 1930s Dutch barge has gorgeous views of the

Houses of Parliament. Bevvies are reasonably priced and – here's the clincher – there's free live gigs. It's first come first served, so make a beeline there early on a sunny day and enjoy the rough-and-ready vibe within earshot of Big Ben.

# PRINCE OF WALES

### Map 5; 467–9 Brixton Road, Brixton; ///cure.narrow.member; www.pow-london.com

Sat atop the Prince of Wales' pub and club, this vast two-tier roof terrace hosts a series of marathon 12-hour parties throughout the summer. It's popular with young Brixtonians plus those drawn from further afield. When the sun's blazing, and you're surrounded by your friends, there are few better places to dance and drink the day – and the night – away. The rooftop views perhaps aren't the best that London has to offer but you'll be having too much fun to care.

Rooftop bars aren't just for summer. Skylight, above Tobacco Dock (www.tobaccodocklondon.com), is at its best in winter, when you can pair a drink with a skate around its adorable ice rink. Forget the rinks at Somerset House and the Natural History Museum – the queues here are smaller, and the views are better, making for a memorable date night. But, if summer's your season, Skylight offers a croquet course during warmer months, perfect for you and your pals.

# Cosy Pubs

*Is there any institution more central to London than the pub? We think not. Nothing is better on a dreary day, when the sun's hiding and all you want is a cosy armchair, a log fire and a glass of something.*

## THE SPANIARDS INN

**Map 6; Spaniards Road, Hampstead; ///tags.deeply.bossy;**
**www.thespaniardshampstead.co.uk**

The Spaniards exudes all the character you'd expect from one of London's oldest inns. The pub has been a Hampstead favourite since 1585 and counts poet Keats among its former regulars. These days, it's the definition of cosy: dogs doze beside their owners, cask ales are enjoyed with hearty roasts, and in the winter the scent of wood smoke drifts from the crackling fire. Perfect after a walk on the heath.

## THE ROYAL OAK

**Map 2; 73 Columbia Road, Bethnal Green; ///valid.social.leap;**
**www.royaloaklondon.com**

Spend a Sunday afternoon roaming along Columbia Road Flower Market and you'll be in full need of a classic, East End pint of ale. This old-school boozer has got you, cramming thirsty punters into its boisterous downstairs bar (more sedate guests head upstairs). Scour the room for a rickety stool or chair and crowd in with the rest of the regulars, who will always make room for a newcomer.

## YE OLDE CHESHIRE CHEESE

**Map 1; 145 Fleet Street, Temple; ///point.track.resist; 020 7353 6170**

Every Londoner knows of Ye Olde Cheshire Cheese, which was rebuilt after the Great Fire of 1666. It's best known for its literary associations – Charles Dickens and Mark Twain were both known to sip on flagons of ale in the pub's warren of dark, low-ceilinged cellar rooms. There's no end of secluded corners to tuck yourself away in, perfect for a date. It's also run by the Samuel Smith Old Brewery, which means that its real ales come at best-value prices.

**»** **Don't leave without** seeking out the taxidermic remains of Polly the Parrot, the pub's foul-mouthed feathered resident, who died in 1926.

## THE HARP

**Map 1; 47 Chandos Place, Covent Garden; ///humans.smoke.blues;**
**www.harpcoventgarden.com**

On a wet and dreary London evening, there are few sights more inviting than the illuminated stained-glass windows of this little London haven. Inside, the welcome is just as warm: squeeze in among the other punters lining the bar and let the genuinely knowledgeable bartenders recommend you a real ale (or two). There's little chance of a seat, but who needs one? Stick close to the bar for good chat and even better beer. It'll be last orders before you know it.

# Solo, Pair, Crowd

**No matter where you are in the city, you're never far from a classic London pub to get snug in.**

### FLYING SOLO

**Get cosy in an old haunt**

The King William IV in Hampstead village has been drawing locals in for 200 years and counting. Draw up a bar stool, order a pint and chat to the barmen – they have many a story to tell.

### IN A PAIR

**Romantic night for two**

Nestle down with a bottle of red on one of the low sofas at The Windmill on Clapham Common. Fingers crossed in-house pup Max joins you both for a snuggle, too.

### FOR A CROWD

**Catch-up by the riverside**

Grab your friends and nab a window spot at Wapping's Captain Kidd. This low-ceilinged riverside pub has lovely views over the Thames, there's always plenty of space and the drinks prices are a steal – perfect for a get-together.

# THE DEVONSHIRE

**Map 6; 39 Balham High Road, Balham; ///prime.feared.guess;
www.devonshirebalham.co.uk**

It might be big but, in the bleak mid-winter, The Devonshire is utterly
snug. Order a pint of bitter, sink down in one of the chesterfields and
keep your fingers crossed that local brass band Dat Brass arrives for
a performance. You'll be warmed up and on your feet in no time.

**» Don't leave without** ordering the baked camembert – the perfect
foodstuff for a cosy evening down the pub.

# THE HALF MOON

**Map 4; 93 Lower Richmond Road, Putney; ///wicked.occupy.fire;
www.halfmoon.co.uk**

This beloved boozer has cemented itself as one of London's best
live music venues – The Rolling Stones, U2 and The Who have all
gigged here. Music aside, it's a lovely place to flop down into a sofa,
and enjoy a pint and pub grub alongside a laid-back crowd.

# THE PALM TREE

**Map 3; Grove Road, Mile End; ///woes.trials.posed; 020 8980 2918**

Standing stalwart on the canal, this boozer is one of the last remaining
to enjoy a proper Cockney knees-up. The décor has little changed in
50 years, likewise the drinks choice hasn't evolved, and the owners still
haven't set up a website. Still, every Friday and Saturday night, locals
congregate for live crooning jazz (just wait for Kerry the barmaid to
take the mic) and the pub feels like a home away from home.

# Breweries and Distilleries

*Yes, London's a city that has long loved drinking booze but it's also one that loves making it. And a growing wave of distilleries and urban wineries are stealing the limelight from beloved craft breweries.*

## BULLFINCH BREWERY

### Map 5; Arches 886–7 Rosendale Road, Herne Hill; ///stud.deep.cages; www.thebullfinchbrewery.co.uk

Set in a railway arch near Brockwell Park, wonderfully unpretentious Bullfinch Brewery will give you all the local community feels; punters shift up to make space, dogs obligingly let you tickle their tummies and the person who'll pull your pint most likely brewed it.

## KANPAI

### Map 5; Unit 2A.2, Copeland Park, 133 Copeland Road, Peckham; ///roses.speeds.spins; www.kanpai.london

Something special has been quietly brewing away in the shadow of Peckham's much loved Bussey Building. The UK's first sake brewery is set in a tiny warehouse; you'll spot the puffs of steam from its fermentation tanks, the warehouse doors flung open whatever the weather. In winter, punters in beanies and thick scarves huddle over steaming bowls of ramen and sip their hot sake; in the summer they spill out onto the pavement with glasses of refreshingly cold sake. Learn all about the art of the Japanese drink on a Saturday brewery tour.

**» Don't leave without** trying a glass of sparkling sake – few people know that this Japanese spirit also comes in a crisp, bubbling form.

## HAWKES CIDERY AND TAP ROOM

**Map 5; 90 Druid Street, Bermondsey; ///funny.swim.fancy; www.wearehawkes.com**

Nestled amid the craft ale sellers on the Bermondsey Beer Mile, Hawkes is something different from its neighbours. For one, it's London's first urban cider brewery. Add to that the fact that it crafts ciders from donated apples and those rejected by supermarkets and you'll see why eco-conscious Londoners love it. The handmade stone-baked pizzas are also a welcome sight for boozy punters.

Off the beaten path, and away from the crowds thronging along Bermondsey Beer Mile, is Walthamstow Beer Mile. Little known, even among Londoners, there's a wonderful neighbourhood community feel in the taprooms here. Breweries includes award-winning Pillar, Wild Card, Exhale and Signature, with more expected to open as hype grows.

## BERMONDSEY DISTILLERY

**Map 5; 55 Stanworth Street, Bermondsey; ///heats.chest.bands;**
**www.bermondseygin.com**

A place that's confidently not trying to do anything new, Bermondsey
Distillery is a love letter to the past. Inspired by London's lost distilleries,
this small-batch place is devoted to traditional gin botanicals.
Under the arches by Maltby Street Market, it opens on weekends
for those wanting to stretch out their market visit with something a
little stronger. Gin aficionados should check out the distillery tours.

## EAST LONDON LIQUOR COMPANY

**Map 3; 221 Grove Road, Bow; ///goal.props.teams;**
**www.eastlondonliquorcompany.com**

In 1903, the Lea Valley Distillery became the last East London
whisky maker to turn off its stills, ending the long history of distilling
in the area. Today, this small producer of whisky, gin, vodka and rum
has reinstated those spirit-making roots. Based in a former glue
factory by the canal in Bow Wharf, the on-site tasting bar always
has plenty of seats and a chilled vibe.

## CRATE BREWERY

**Map 6; Unit 7, Queens Yard, Hackney; ///gone.panels.fund;**
**www.cratebrewery.com**

Crate is a cavernous former print factory with craft beers on tap,
industrial canalside views, and a sea of beards and tattoos – yes, this
place is peak hipster but it pulls it off well. And on sunny days – when

Earn your pint by arriving by kayak, with Secret Adventures. Trips along London's oldest canal start at Limehouse Basin.

the crowds sprawl along the canalside, narrowboats tootle past and the DJ hits their stride – there's nowhere better to be. A pizzeria is on hand to feed the masses and a zero-waste kitchen is in the works.

## HACKNEY CHURCH BREW CO.

**Map 3; 16–17 Bohemia Place, Hackney; ///first.bound.glass;
www.hackneychurchbrew.co**

It might be little but this Hackney brewpub packs a punch. The on-tap brews span crisp IPAs to chocolatey stouts, all designed to please the palates of Hackney's craft beer addicts who carry their freshly pulled pints carefully back to their mates, careful not to spill a precious drop. Better yet, most of the brewing ingredients are sourced within a stone's throw of the brewery, showing off its community focus.

## RENEGADE LONDON WINERY

**Map 2; Arch 12, Gales Gardens, Bethnal Green; ///moving.silves.shark;
www.renegadelondonwine.com**

London's concrete jungle isn't the first place you'd think to open a winery but as the English wine scene blossoms, urban wineries are starting to pop up here. Renegade, East London's first winery, turns the best grapes from England and Europe into experimental new blends. Its wine bar, set in a railway arch dotted with candlelit tables, barrels and fermentation tanks, is a brilliant place to sample its produce. On balmy nights head to the lovely outdoor terrace.

CITY OF
LONDON

**Admire the view from**
## THE OLD THAMESIDE INN
This former spice warehouse was
converted into an inn, its position by the
Thames ideal for delivering goods. Sip a
pint here and enjoy the riverside locale.

BANKSIDE

Thames

PARK ST

TOOLEY STREET

ST THOMAS STREET

**①**

**②**

**Soak up history at**
## THE GEORGE INN
Stop by the city's only surviving
coaching inn – which dates
back to medieval times – to
admire its galleried façade
and tuck into a hearty pie.

DRUID STREET

JAMAICA ROAD

**③**

**Snoop around at**
## JENSEN'S GIN
## DISTILLERY
Bermondsey was "London's Larder"
in the 19th century, storing produce
in its many warehouses. Today
Jensen's uses one for the distillation
of gin, based on an 1840s recipe.
Take a tour to find out more.

BERMONDSE

ENID STREET

LUCEY

SOUTHWARK PARK R

0 metres        500
0 yards         500

# An afternoon of
# **brewing history**

This is a city built on brewing. The 18th century saw the development of a dark, hoppy beer called porter – so-called because river porters in particular used to enjoy it – which made London the UK's most important brewing city. Technological advances aided production and the popularity of porter made Southwark, just south of the Thames, a centre of beer-making in the 19th century. Despite a decline in independent brewers in the 20th century, London has seen a brewery boom since the noughties, with some of the city's best artisanal breweries and gin distilleries centred in Bermondsey, right next door to Southwark.

SHADWELL

WAPPING

**Bermondsey Beer Mile** *perfectly embodies London's modern craft beer revolution. The stretch of microbreweries opens on Saturdays.*

RAYMOUTH ROAD

**4**

**Pop into PARTIZAN**

Partizan has been brewing since 2012. Grab a table in its makeshift tap room and round off your tour with a zesty double-hopped IPA.

SOUTH BERMONDSEY

**1. The Old Thameside Inn**
Pickfords Wharf, Borough;
www.nicholsonspubs.co.uk;
///pencil.bunch.organ

**2. The George Inn**
75–7 Borough High
Street, Southwark;
www.greeneking-pubs.co.uk;
///tuned.region.tulip

**3. Jensen's Gin Distillery**
55 Stanworth Street,
Bermondsey; www.
bermondseygin.com;
///buns.camera.dreams

**4. Partizan**
34 Raymouth Road,
Bermondsey; www.
partizanbrewing.co.uk;
///most.cherry.sprint

**Bermondsey Beer Mile** ///brief.less.feel

# SHOP

*Shopping is woven into the lives of Londoners: markets shape weekends, vintage boutiques update wardrobes and book nooks offer the next gripping read for the commute.*

# Vintage Gems

*London has long loved vintage, and the retro revolution continues to make waves. Stalwarts of the scene, like Portobello Market – famed for its antique curiosities – are now rivalled by an abundance of second-hand boutiques and emporiums.*

## ALADDIN'S CAVE

**Map 6; 72 Loampit Hill, Lewisham; ///punch.peanut.truly; 020 8320 2553**
An aptly named warren of wonders, this crumbling former railway station is one of London's more bizarre shopping experiences, loved by expert and newbie treasure seekers alike. Furniture explodes onto the pavement – wicker chairs, time-worn sofas and claw-foot bathtubs, all making a bid to escape the clutches of this eclectic store. Inside, items are stacked to the ceiling, blocking out the daylight.

## OLD SPITALFIELDS MARKET

**Map 2; 16 Horner Square, Shoreditch; ///fetch.herb.engine;**
**www.oldspitalfieldsmarket.com**
Old Spitalfields, the original East London market, might be hemmed in with gleaming stores but the locals keep coming back for all the olden knick-knacks. Old boys in flat caps and cool kids in bucket hats

rummage in unison through vintage maps and well-thumbed books. There's a vinyl market for music lovers on the first and third Friday of the month, while all other days see traders selling everything from handmade clothing and art to artisan soaps.

## PORTOBELLO ROAD MARKET
### Map 4; Portobello Road, Notting Hill; ///bath.raced.models; www.portobelloroad.co.uk

Photogenic pastel-hued buildings, vintage dresses swaying in the breeze, the lyrical cries of traders to a wonderfully diverse crowd – visiting Portobello Road is a quintessential London activity, albeit a bit of a scrum. There's a market here every day but Saturdays are when things are most lively: tables overflow with bundles of fresh fruit and veg, smoke rises from street food stalls and rickety tables are littered with all manner of pre-loved curiosities.

**»** **Don't leave without** seeing the Banksy mural near the corner of Portobello Road and Acklam Road.

## 2&4 VINTAGE RETRO FURNITURE
### Map 3; 2–4 Southgate Road, Hackney; ///tiles.bars.piles; 020 7254 5202

Stylish couples frequent this little boutique, running their fingers along polished mid-20th-century furniture while French bulldogs wait patiently at their feet. The speciality here is restored Danish pieces from the 1950s to the 1970s, and the sleek wood surfaces, rounded corners and muted tones are a calming treat for the eyes – just imagine if your house could look like that, too.

# PAPER DRESS VINTAGE

### Map 3; 352a Mare Street, Hackney; ///rocket.fund.insert; www.paperdressvintage.co.uk

This sustainable boutique by Hackney Central station goes by the simple mantra: clothing from the past was built to last, so why waste your money on fast fashion? Pop in to browse vintage garb spanning the 20th century, with retro-styled staff on hand to help you find your look. Come nighttime, platform heels are swapped for trainers when the shop is transformed into a live music and event space.

# BEYOND RETRO

### Map 3; 92–100 Stoke Newington Road, Dalston; ///king.that.system; www.beyondretro.com

Whichever area of London you're in, you'll see groups of teens and 20-somethings decked out in 1990s athleisure wear, pre-loved aviator jackets and vibrantly patterned headscarves. Chances are these fashion gems were picked up at Beyond Retro, a name revered by London's vintage shoppers. This particular treasure trove

## Try it!
## FASHION FIX UP

Got a pair of vintage jeans that need a little TLC? Get your stitch on at Fabrications on Broadway Market. The shop runs various upcycling and garment repair workshops with the friendliest crafting experts.

has more than 12,000 unique pieces, from sparkly flapper dresses to retro American sweaters. You won't be able to get away without at least one plaid shirt – you've been warned.

>> **Don't leave without** checking out the shop's reworked vintage range. The fit or style has been retailored to match modern runway trends.

## ANNIE'S

**Map 2; 12 Camden Passage, Islington; ///tested.member.march;**
**www.anniesvintageclothing.co.uk**

Annie's is the doyenne of London's vintage shopping, attracting serious fashionistas in search of old-world glamour (Kate Moss frequents this jewel of a store). Beautifully curated and with an air of decadence, this is the place to unearth the wedding dress of your dreams or a gown for a fancy work event. There's also a bargain rail for those who want to leave with a little piece of vintage for just a few pounds.

## BRICK LANE VINTAGE MARKET

**Map 2; 85 Brick Lane, Shoreditch; ///feel.points.clear;**
**www.vintage-market.co.uk**

East London and vintage shopping go hand in hand, thanks to the area's wonderfully rich history and its famously creative residents. Just look at The Old Truman Brewery – once the city's largest brewery and today the home of Brick Lane Vintage Market. Every day of the week, stallholders with an eye for style cram their vintage wares into the weathered warehouse, with hipsters quick to comb the rails for feather capes, leather jackets and dapper suits.

# Record Shops

*London is a city rippling with musical history, and
this is celebrated in its record shops. Surely there is
nothing more rewarding than unearthing an elusive
album or dusting off a classic vinyl to take home?*

## LITTLE RECORD SHOP

**Map 6; 43 Tottenham Lane, Crouch End; ///clouds.racks.spit;
www.cash4records.co.uk**

You're in safe hands at this North London gem, where vinyl collector
David has been buying and selling records for over 15 years. Here
you'll find rare collections of prog rock, folk, 1950s jazz, northern
soul, funk, post-punk – whatever you're hankering after, he's got it.
Better still, he offers fairer prices than you'll find elsewhere. Join
other music fans in making this your number-one calling point.

## AUDIO GOLD

**Map 6; 308–10 Park Road, Muswell Hill; ///prompting.surely.twice;
www.audiogold.co.uk**

Audio Gold by name and by nature; this Muswell Hill haven is the
place to visit if you're getting into vinyl or looking to upgrade. Few
other places have such a chocolate box of audio equipment, starting

with wind-up gramophones and extending to second-hand hi-fis from the 1980s and 1990s — the heyday of musical manufacturing. Make use of the staff's sage advice and try out anything before you buy.

**» Don't leave without** scanning the room for UK music royalty; BBC radio regulars in particular love Audio Gold.

# ROUGH TRADE EAST

### Map 2; Truman Brewery, Brick Lane; ///exit.turned.supply; www.roughtrade.com

The Rough Trade label became a household name among UK musos when it signed The Smiths in the early 1980s. Now, it's known for this vast record store and gig space, where a purpose-built stage hosts album debuts. The range of CDs and vinyl on offer is huge: you'll come for your favourite band's latest release and leave hours later with three or four other records in tow that you never knew you needed. It's a must-visit for anyone exploring Brick Lane.

Keep an eye out for the Rough Trade gig listings (www. roughtrade.com/gb/events). Entry is usually free with the purchase of the album that's being promoted, and though sets are shorter than in bigger gig spaces, they're much more intimate. Some unexpectedly big names have performed here, too; Radiohead played a surprise six-song set in 2008. Who will be the next big band or artist to perform?

# FLASHBACK RECORDS

**Map 2; 50 Essex Road, Islington; ///clear.rider.tries; www.flashback.co.uk**

Old rockers and young ravers unite at the entrance to Flashback, wooed by the bargain buckets of records by the front door. Pass through the ground floor dedicated to CDs and find the vinyl-only room downstairs, where you'll see serious music fans search for unique samples of rare jazz, hip hop and soul. There's even another branch of Flashback Records on Brick Lane if you need a second hit.

**>> Don't leave without** enquiring about the store's events programme, dedicated to the artists signed to the Flashback Records label.

# RECKLESS RECORDS

**Map 1; 30 Berwick Street, Soho; ///shared.ranged.piles; www.reckless.co.uk**

Nostalgia calls at this family-run shop, which has been buying and selling small record collections for over 40 years. After a bit of 1960s prog? They've got it. Drum and bass more your thing? That's here too. In short: this place has a pleasing amount of everything. It's hardly surprising that music lovers adore it; after all, it even featured on the cover of Oasis album *(What's the Story) Morning Glory?*

# PHONICA

**Map 1; 51 Poland Street, Soho; ///rats.finely.stores; www.phonicarecords.com**

Movers and shakers gravitate toward this dance vinyl specialist, where stacks of minimal techno and nu disco are flaunted beside dubstep and French electro – arguably, the shop's most impressive section. Speak to the uber-cool staff about the Phonica Records label, Record Store Day parties and live streams – all different ways to worship at the altar of dance music. You might even find yourself next to DJ regulars Four Tet, Floating Points or Caribou.

## MUSIC AND VIDEO EXCHANGE

**Map 4; 38 Notting Hill Gate, Notting Hill; ///trails.cases.reward; www.mgeshops.com**

Since 1967 this place has been categorizing and flogging crates of pre-loved vinyl records and CDs. The Exchange is constantly unearthing well-thumbed records to sell on, which means an ever-evolving stock; a selection you see on a Monday could be completely different by Friday. This means two things: you must snap up a bargain the moment you see it, and you must come back to visit as often as possible. You won't be the only one – some hardcore regulars at this shop come back several times a day.

## KRISTINA RECORDS

**Map 3; 194 Well Street, Homerton; ///each.plant.scales; www.kristinarecords.com**

This independent crate-diggers' mecca based in South Hackney specializes in weird and wonderful avant-garde releases. The whole vibe is cool and modern, which beckons to younger music fans who are on the hunt for dance music gems or a new set of mixing decks. The staff are uber knowledgeable and more than happy to recommend a record or two; you'll find yourself picking their brains over a coffee in the shop café.

# Book Nooks

*Bookshops are cornerstones of their neighbourhoods: beautifully curated shops where children's first books are bought, cosy corners offer refuge and travel adventures are dreamed up.*

## DAUNT BOOKS

### Map 1; 83–4 Marylebone High Street, Marylebone; ///supporter.hardly.entry; www.dauntbooks.co.uk

Edwardian store Daunts is the most beautiful place to browse: soaring ceilings, ornate windows and row upon row of tomes. It's not strictly a travel bookshop but has long been seen as a travel specialist; the stacks of guidebooks will spark wanderlust in the most casual browser.

## RYE BOOKS

### Map 5; 47 North Cross Road, East Dulwich; ///milky.cute.forgot; www.ryebooks.co.uk

Blink and you could miss Rye Books but you really don't want to. An expertly curated selection of books line the walls, labradoodle George snoozes by the counter and the smell of freshly brewed coffee fills the air. The lovely staff are also founts of bookish knowledge and are only too happy to recommend a delicious read for your journey home.

## GAY'S THE WORD

**Map 1; 66 Marchmont Street, Bloomsbury; ///packet.lanes.tennis;**
**www.gaystheword.co.uk**

This was the UK's first gay and lesbian bookstore when it opened in 1979 and continues to stand proud. A dedicated LGBTQ+ following love Gay's The Word for its prize-winning fiction and cutting-edge queer theory. There's also a busy calendar of inclusive discussion groups and events that adds to the community spirit.

## WORD ON THE WATER

**Map 1; Regent's Canal Towpath, Kings Cross; ///exists.gazed.junior;**
**www.wordonthewater.co.uk**

Bobbing on the Regent's Canal amid the rejuvenated grit of King's Cross, this wonderfully quirky floating bookshop is an unmissable spot for bookworms. The 1920s Dutch barge is packed with old and new books, crammed onto its deck and smuggled into its hull.

**» Don't leave without** checking out upcoming events: bookish discussions, live music, open-mic nights and slam poetry evenings.

## STANFORDS

**Map 1; 7 Mercer Walk, Covent Garden; ///stable.marble.couple;**
**www.stanfords.co.uk**

We admit it, we're biased, but it's hard to resist a bookshop dedicated to travel, adventure and escapism. Since it was established in 1853, Stanfords has become the go-to destination for backpackers researching their next adventure and armchair travellers alike.

## Liked by the locals

"Burley Fisher is a community. We run regular events and stock a lot of books and zines by small and independent publishers. Online stores may be convenient, but it will never replicate the pleasure of browsing a well-curated bookshop."

SAM FISHER, CO-FOUNDER AT BURLEY FISHER BOOKS

## BROADWAY BOOKSHOP

**Map 3; 6 Broadway Market, Hackney; ///vibe.label.detect;
www.broadwaybookshophackney.com**

The warmth of jolly owner and book lover Jane pervades this small,
imaginatively stocked place. Broadway Bookshop captivates you
the minute you walk in: hand-picked fiction, reprints of forgotten
gems and well-thumbed classics all have a home here.

**» Don't leave without** calling in at Donlon Books, a specialist
boutique for quirky and out-of-print books, just down the road.

## NEW BEACON BOOKS

**Map 6; 76 Stroud Green Road, Finsbury Park; ///handy.owners.dent;
www.newbeaconbooks.com**

In 2017 the local community rallied around this bookshop, raising
funds to save it from closure and protect it from the onslaught of the
digital age. It's a place worth treasuring – this was the UK's first
Black bookshop when it opened in 1966, and has been celebrating
African and Caribbean voices and literature ever since.

## BURLEY FISHER BOOKS

**Map 3; 400 Kingsland Road, Dalston; ///atom.ants.nature;
www.burleyfisherbooks.com**

Edgy East Enders study tomes through their round tortoise-shell
glasses at this indie treasure trove. It's all about small-press books and
community spirit at Burley Fisher, which is best experienced with a
glass of red at a literary event in the popular basement bar.

# Home Touches

*Londoners love personalizing their homes, whether that's with a jungle of plants, jazzily coloured soft furnishings or locally crafted pottery. And you can buy a bit of London to take home too.*

## FOREST

**Map 5; Rear of 43 Lordship Lane, East Dulwich;///ticket.parade.slurs; www.forest.london**

You'd struggle to find a Londoner who doesn't have a luscious fern or pot of ivy draped across their desk or window sill. Those living south of the river turn to Forest – a tiny, tropical nook of a plant shop packed with little armies of cacti and succulents waiting patiently for a new

Open by appointment only, Pentreath and Hall *(www.pentreath-hall.com)* is often overlooked, even by locals. Around the corner from Lamb's Conduit Street – a lovely stretch of independents – this shop is packed with colourful accessories for the home, including prints and cushions.

home. If you can't pack a plant, don't fret; there's a beautiful collection of lifestyle products tucked amid the greenery, including brass-rimmed photo frames, decorative cushions and gorgeous crockery.

# HOUSE OF HACKNEY

### Map 2; 131 Shoreditch High Street, Shoreditch; ///rabble.drag.chats; www.houseofhackney.com

Forget Liberty – there's a new kid on the block. House of Hackney prides itself on dishing out a bit of affordable luxury for the home, thanks to its stock of print-based and heritage-inspired homewares. Attracting artsy Londoners hunting for that next striking piece for their city abode, here you'll find rugs, cushions and lamps, all in a glorious, hedonistic splash of colour. There's also a focus on craftsmanship, with products made in England using local, sustainable materials.

# NUNHEAD GARDENER

### Map 5; 1a Oakdale Road, Nunhead; ///nods.simply.filled; www.thenunheadgardener.com

Run by Peter Milne and his husband Alex Beltran, who both quit their city jobs to follow their true passion for plants, the Nunhead Gardener is not your run-of-the-mill garden centre. In these two railway archways green-fingered retirees hobnob with trendy young professionals, all foraging through the succulents, cacti and glazed pots for something to brighten their homes.

>> **Don't leave without** strolling up the hill for a walk through the eerily beautiful, forested pathways of Nunhead Cemetery.

# CORNERCOPIA

**Map 6; 63 Streatham Hill, Streatham; ///views.jars.dwell;**
**www.cornercopiastore.co.uk**

This shop is the favourite snoozing spot of Ginger the Cornercopia cat, and it's easy to see why. Cornercopia is like a rustically cosy home, thanks to its shelves laden with gorgeous — and often locally made — homeware items. Think lambswool blankets, pastel-coloured candlesticks and hand-crafted wooden utensils.

**»** **Don't leave without** browsing the enticing homeware collection in boutique store Lark, just down the hill from Cornercopia.

# PRICK

**Map 3; 492 Kingsland Road, Dalston; ///basis.move.curving;**
**www.prickldn.com**

London's first boutique dedicated solely to cacti and succulents, Prick was a labour of love for plant provocateur Gynelle Leon, who quit her job and sold her home to launch the shop. Fortunately for those who keep killing off their desk plants, Gynelle is on hand with advice and a handy selection of foliage-themed books.

# GOD'S OWN JUNKYARD

**Map 6; Unit 12, Ravenswood Industrial Estate, Shernall Street,**
**Walthamstow; ///themes.intent.nets; www.godsownjunkyard.co.uk**

This psychedelic store is a must-visit, whether or not you're in the market for some neon home lighting. Accessed via a nondescript car park, God's Own Junkyard is truly eye-watering, thanks to the vintage neon street signs, disco balls and kitsch memorabilia that cover every single surface. You can feel a bit woozy in all that neon glare; fortunately the in-house coffee shop is at arm's length – perfect for regaining your balance over a brew.

## THE CONRAN SHOP

**Map 1; 55 Marylebone High Street, Marylebone; ///soak.cross.entry; www.conranshop.co.uk**

Expect to mingle with a well-dressed clientele in this iconic London homeware store. The Conran Shop is renowned for its colourful collections of swanky homeware that hit all the current design and homeware trends. Even if you're just casually browsing the cushions, glassware, candles or stationery, something will make its way into your shopping basket; you've been warned.

## CONSERVATORY ARCHIVES

**Map 3; 493–5 Hackney Road, Hackney; ///fall.broke.rather; www.conservatoryarchives.co.uk**

Vast windows, faded tiles and bare plaster walls form the backdrop to the main event here: a jungle of tropical plants. When it opened in 2015, Conservatory Archives was the first indoor plant store in the UK, spearheading a growing obsession with adopting plant babies for our homes. Interspersed with mid-20th-century furniture, a lush tangle of greenery greets visitors: foliage-draped hanging baskets, the sprawling leaves of cheese plants and row upon row of bulbous succulents. It's all great fodder for a social media feed.

# Beloved Markets

*London's markets are at the core of city life. From crack-of-dawn butchers supplying restaurants to weekend markets where locals browse artisan goods, these city stalwarts keep the capital humming.*

## BROADWAY MARKET

### Map 3; Broadway Market, London Fields; ///shirts.sketch.wished; www.broadwaymarket.co.uk

On Saturdays this Hackney street houses London's hippest market. A fruit and veg market has been on the site since the 1890s, and food is still the main draw – young families and groups of flatmates browse the artisan cheeses, baked goods and mounds of fresh produce to take home. Food aside, there's plenty else to buy, from vintage clothes to fresh blooms to handmade crafts.

## COLUMBIA ROAD FLOWER MARKET

### Map 2; Columbia Road, Hackney; ///afford.love.petty; www.columbiaroad.info

For many Londoners, Columbia Road is the perfect Sunday day out and a remaining slice of East London, where the sing-song of traders' cockney rhyming slang rings out above the crowds. Sure, some will recommend you arrive early to beat the rush, but we say where's the fun in that? Hit the street at midday, coffee in hand from a local independent, and shuffle along with the rest of them, pausing to treat yourself to a bouquet of beautiful blooms.

**»** **Don't leave without** stocking up on pots for your leafy purchases from the brilliantly named Stoned & Plastered, just off Columbia Road.

## SMITHFIELDS MEAT MARKET

**Map 2; Charterhouse Street, City of London; ///rich.owner.supper;**
**www.smithfieldmarket.com**

Housed in three listed buildings, this is the largest wholesale meat market in the UK. Things kick off early here, with the gates swinging open at 2am on weekdays to savvy restaurateurs, city butchers and meat-fiends with an eye for a bargain. In the moonlight the market hums: white-cloaked porters frantically steer rattling pallet trucks and the jovial banter of long-time traders fills the air.

## NEW COVENT GARDEN FLOWER MARKET

**Map 4; Nine Elms Lane, Nine Elms; ///scope.fancy.guilty;**
**www.newcoventgardenmarket.com**

This historic flower market has hopped between many homes since 1670 and has now settled in a site by the redeveloped Battersea Power Station, which is perfect for those looking to grab a well-earned breakfast after browsing the market. Things kick off at 4am (every day bar Sunday) but the bargain blooms make the early start worth it.

# Solo, Pair, Crowd

**Barter best alone? Fancy hitting the stalls with some friends? There's a London market to suit every need.**

## FLYING SOLO
### A bloom of one's own
Packed to the brim, Columbia Road Market is best navigated alone. Battle off the competition, then reward your bargaining skills with a coffee and baked good from Jones Dairy Café.

## IN A PAIR
### Village vibes and private picnics
Browse Greenwich Market's bustling stalls and grab some street food or picnic supplies before popping over to wonderfully leafy Greenwich Park. The views across the Thames aren't too terrible, either.

## FOR A CROWD
### Market goods and rooftop booze
London's hippest market, Broadway Market is the perfect place for a group exploration – finish up with rooftop views and drinks at nearby Netil360 *(p74)*.

## BRIXTON VILLAGE AND MARKET ROW
**Map 5; Atlantic Road, Brixton; ///teach.evenly.cape;
www.wearebrixtonvillage.co.uk**

Straddling the frenetic scene of Atlantic Road are Brixton Village and Market Row, a duo of covered markets that symbolize the soul of Black Britain. Gentrification has seen chain pizza places and chichi boutiques replace much-loved family-run Afro-Caribbean stores and bakeries; this is London with all its complexities. The markets have been the subject of much discussion over the years – all the more reason to visit and show your support to the original small businesses.

## CAMDEN MARKET
**Map 1; Camden Lock Place; ///highs.latter.puzzle; www.camdenmarket.com**

You can't miss this market – it's under a huge "The Camden Market" sign. Before that you'll see crowds of grungy teens and bearded hipsters thronging along Camden Lock, looking to spend their money on vintage clothing, quirky art, Gothic jewellery and more besides.

## HERNE HILL MARKET
**Map 5; Railton Road, Herne Hill; ///form.likely.curry; 020 8293 6436**

A stone's throw from Brockwell Park, this market is a great Sunday activity. Supporting locally produced food and crafts, it's infused with Herne Hill's villagey vibe: families stock up on fresh veg, independents line the streets and locals play ditties on the communal piano.

**» Don't leave without** popping into Herne Hill Books, where the latest bestsellers share shelf space with with timeless classics.

# An afternoon of
# vintage shopping

Once the poorest quarter of the city, East London is today the most creative – you only need to look at the locals' fashion to realize. The likes of Shoreditch and Spitalfields are breeding grounds for well-priced vintage stores selling pre-loved vinyl, clothing and homeware. Start on Brick Lane, featuring one of the most renowned clusters of second-hand vendors in the UK, before walking up to Hackney and finishing the day with some pints at a classic East End boozer.

**1. Poppie's**
6-8 Hanbury Street, Spitalfields; www.poppies fishandchips.co.uk;
///clocks.both.wiring

**2. Brick Lane Vintage Market**
85 Brick Lane, Shoreditch; www.vintage-market.co.uk;
///feels.points.clear

**3. Rough Trade East**
91 Brick Lane, Shoreditch; www.roughtrade.com;
///exit.turned.supply

**4. Rokit**
101/107 Brick Lane, Shoreditch; www.rokit.co.uk;
///tones.polite.live

**5. The Birdcage**
80 Columbia Road, Hackney; www.draft house.co.uk;
///rank.spit.highs

 **The Well and Bucket**
///dragon.mime.grant

HOXTON

OLD STREET

GREAT EASTERN STREET

Liverpool Stree Station

BISHOPSGATE

**Columbia Road**, *today a haven for vintage shops, was once home to a food market for the poor set up by philanthropist Angela Burdett-Coutts in 1896.*

*Ion Square Gardens*

COLUMBIA RD

**5** Rest your feet at
**THE BIRDCAGE**

Order a drink in the historical Birdcage, or "The Birdy" to locals. If you're lucky, you might even catch a live gig.

COLUMBIA RD

VIRGINIA ROAD

SWANFIELD STREET

*Weaver's Fields*

*Standing stalwart,* **The Well and Bucket** *is one of the East End's oldest pubs, having first opened in 1818. The tiling inside shows the pub's age.*

BETHNAL GREEN ROAD

SHOREDITCH HIGH STREET

**SHOREDITCH**

SCLATER ST

CHESHIRE ST

BRICK LANE

**Make a detour to
ROUGH TRADE EAST**

Electronica fan? Prefer punk, or funk? Whatever music you like, chances are you'll find it in Rough Trade East's vintage vinyl section.

**4** Pop into
**ROKIT**

You'll find a bargain at Rokit, like a second-hand denim jacket or perhaps an 80s jumpsuit.

**3**

**SPITALFIELDS**

**1** HANBURY ST

**2** Peruse the rails at
**BRICK LANE
VINTAGE MARKET**

Try on pre-loved Doc Martens and military-style coats at this indoor market, where vintage specialists sell clothing from the 1920s onwards.

**Lunch at
POPPIE'S**

Grab a table by the jukebox and tuck into a parcel of fish and chips at this white-tiled, family-run chippie.

BISHOPSGATE

BRICK LANE

**WHITECHAPEL**

| 0 metres | 250 |
| 0 yards | 250 |

# ARTS & CULTURE

*London is a cultural colossus. Cavernous museums tell the vital stories of the past, while indie galleries and striking street murals comment on the present and future.*

# City History

*The UK and its capital have been shaped by people, so it should only follow that its museums celebrate the richness of our shared past. These small but mighty institutions are a great starting point.*

## LONDON TRANSPORT MUSEUM

**Map 1; Covent Garden Piazza, Covent Garden; ///that.overnight.goad; www.ltmuseum.co.uk**

Buried beneath London is another world: sealed-off Tube stations, crumbling tunnels and abandoned platforms. It's a world that the young families enthusiastically exploring the old Tubes and buses here know nothing about. Impress your own parents and book onto the museum's exclusive Hidden London tours, where you'll uncover lost spaces, such as bomb shelters used by Londoners in World War II.

## MUSEUM OF LONDON DOCKLANDS

**Map 6; 1 Warehouse, West India Quay, Canary Wharf; ///puppy.sweep. ranged; www.museumoflondon.org.uk**

The West India Docks were the world's largest dock complex when they opened in 1802 and this museum, in the shadow of Canary Wharf's modern skyscrapers, looks at how these historical warehouses

Cross the quay bridge to Crossrail Place Roof Garden, home to plants from across the globe – perfect for an afternoon's stroll.

operated. Here you'll discover the stories of merchants and pirates, the trade of enslaved African people and sugar, and the uncomfortable resulting success of the British economy and empire.

## THE POSTAL MUSEUM

**Map 1; 15–20 Phoenix Place, Clerkenwell; ///being.orange.vouch;**
**www.postalmuseum.org**

Okay, a visit to a postal museum doesn't sound like the most exciting of days out but this sorting office genuinely brings to life five fascinating centuries of postal work in the city. Learn how Royal Mail grew from a handful of messengers who delivered notes from the king into an integral nationwide service. The true highlight is the chance to ride on the city's secret postal railway, a 100-year-old subterranean train that transported packages and letters across the capital.

**»  Don't leave without** grabbing a bite to eat at foodie-favourite Exmouth Market, which is a mere five-minute walk away.

## THE JEWISH MUSEUM

**Map 1; 129–31 Albert Street, Camden; ///limes.format.dizzy;**
**www.jewishmuseum.org.uk**

East London was traditionally the heartland of Jewish settlement in the UK though today communities live in all corners of the city. This expansive museum reflects the experiences of Jewish Londoners and houses important Holocaust and anti-racist exhibitions.

## DENNIS SEVERS' HOUSE

**Map 2; 18 Folgate Street, Spitalfields; ///dine.ants.panel;**

**www.dennissevershouse.co.uk**

London has long been a city of immigrants. Take the French Huguenots, who moved en masse to cheap and cheerful Spitalfields in the 17th century. Artist Dennis Severs transports you to that time at 18 Folgate Street with an intimate imagined portrait of family life. It's adults only and particularly popular with cuddled-up couples.

## RAGGED SCHOOL MUSEUM

**Map 6; 46–50 Copperfield Road, Bow; ///decks.ally.swaps;**

**www.raggedschoolmuseum.org.uk**

On the first Sunday of every month, you can subject yourself and your pals to a potentially traumatic experience – a reenactment of a Victorian school lesson. Ragged schools provided tuition, food

Want to see London from a different perspective? Unseen Tours *(www.unseentours.org.uk)* do just this, highlighting the hidden stories and secrets around the likes of Shoreditch, Soho and Covent Garden. Even better, this is a social enterprise with tours led by formerly homeless Londoners. You could explore Shoreditch with Henri the humorist, Soho with knowledgeable Nic or Covent Garden with "Vivepedia." (Seriously, Viv knows everything about the local area.)

and clothes for impoverished children in the Victorian East End and this building was once the largest in London. Interesting fact: it was set up by Dr Barnardo, a radical anti-child-poverty activist.

## BLACK HISTORY WALK

**Map 2; Tower Hill underground station, Tower Hill; ///year.space.goats; www.blackhistorywalks.co.uk**

Brush up on London's often-ignored Black history by booking yourself and your friends onto a Black History Walk. Designed by founder Tony Warner, the walks – which cover 12 areas of the city – bring a more rounded world-view to the many London tours on offer. We suggest the Black History Walk in Tower Hamlets to get you started; you'll learn all about London Docklands' history of slavery before ending up at the Museum of London Docklands *(p112)*.

## EAST END WOMEN'S MUSEUM

**Map 6; Abbey Green, Barking; www.eastendwomensmuseum.org**

In 2015, a proposed women's history museum in East London instead opened as a museum dedicated to notorious serial killer Jack the Ripper. Huge uproar ensued, culminating in a Kickstarter campaign to fund this museum, which is dedicated to the research, writing and telling of women's stories via exhibitions, events and workshops. The museum is opening in a brand spanking new space in Barking in 2021; visit with your girlfriends and celebrate girl power.

**» Don't leave without** getting the inside line on monuments to women's history that can be visited across London.

# Street Art

*London has long been home to colour-splashed streets. From famous pieces by graffiti giants to ever-evolving tunnels where newer artists practise their craft – there's always something different to see.*

## LEAKE STREET TUNNEL

**Map 5; Leake Street, Waterloo; ///quest.energetic.rested; www.leakestreetarches.london**

The constantly changing Leake Street Tunnel is one of the best spots to catch street art in the making. Since Banksy put it on the map with the 2008 Festival of the Cans, this 300-m tunnel has become a go-to for practising artists, especially taggers who paint joyful pieces that you'll want to snap and share. The tunnel is transformed from day to day – usually a fresh piece of work from the morning will already have been sprayed over by nightfall.

## RIVINGTON STREET

**Map 2; Rivington Street, Shoreditch; ///moves.owls.impose**

The first thing you notice on a visit to Shoreditch is the colour-splashed streets. In fact, there's such a wealth on show that it can be hard to know where to focus your attention. To see the best of it, head

The Shoreditch Street Art Tours, led by photographer David, are a great way to see more *(www.shoreditch streetarttours.co.uk)*.

to Rivington Street, where you'll see the stick figures synonymous with local artist Stik and the striking *Scary* mural by Eine, which is intended to poke fun at those who feel a naive fear at the sight of graffiti.

# BRICK LANE

### Map 2; Brick Lane, Shoreditch; ///trades.walk.custom

The bricks of Brick Lane have many stories to tell: Bengali street signs signal the area's history of immigration, peeling posters hint at political leanings and street murals provide a social commentary. A tour here gives a great snapshot of local life. After all, London's hoi polloi love to meander here, stopping on their day's errands to take in longstanding artworks by urban art legends D-Face, ROA and Omar Hassan and those by newer artists looking for their big break.

**» Don't leave without** pausing mid-tour for a drink in Montys Bar, surrounded by vivid murals on all sides.

# KENTISH TOWN ROAD

### Map 1; Kentish Town Road, Camden; ///chained.claps.views

Camden's famously vibrant street art lives on. One of the best pockets is Kentish Town Road, where tattoo junkies in Doc Martens parade alongside colourful and abstract murals. While in the area, duck into adjoining Hawley Road to see the giant mural of an aerosol spraying fire and to nearby Camden Road for the unmissable portrait of Camden icon Amy Winehouse.

# BRIXTON STREET ART

### Map 5; Brixton; ///pink.anyone.crowned

Buzzing, non-stop Brixton is home to some of South London's best and most politicized urban art. Here you'll discover iconic works that date back to the 1970s and 80s, such as the much-tagged-over Nuclear Dawn Mural on Carlton Mansions, as well as more modern anti-gentrification pieces. The Save the Brixton Arches campaign, established in 2015, united local street artists who supported local businesses battling eviction from the railway arches along Atlantic Road. Pick up a coffee and visit early in the morning when the shop shutters are still down, revealing these heartfelt and powerful artworks.

» **Don't leave without** checking out the David Bowie mural on Tunstall Road, just around the corner from the singer's birthplace.

# FISH ISLAND

### Map 6; Fish Island, Hackney; ///uses.flight.call

This industrial-turned-artsy hub is where East London's coolest come for a canalside walk of a weekend. Set in creatively minded Hackney, Fish Island is dotted with artist's studios but many taggers prefer to try out new styles on the streets and waterside pathways. Start near Hackney Wick's overground station and head down mural-plastered White Post Lane. Grab a takeaway pint from Crate Brewery (p82) and stroll along the River Lea Navigation to the likes of Stour Road, Smeed Road and the aptly named Bream Street and Dace Road for artworks galore. Or if you want to see taggers hard at work with their spray cans, the towpath at Hertford Union Lock is a good bet.

## Liked by the locals

"Street art and graffiti are essential to our society. They're a form of expression that gives everyone and anyone an opportunity to have their views heard – political and social. It's a vital medium of expression, and London more than anywhere else has really embraced that."

USAMAH KISE, STREET ARTIST

# Favourite Museums

*Thanks to their fame, London's encyclopaedic
museums can get crowded. But there are ways to
experience these cultural powerhouses in relative
peace and with a difference.*

## NATURAL HISTORY MUSEUM

**Map 4; Cromwell Road, South Kensington; ///encounter.poems.magic;
www.nhm.ac.uk**

While wide-eyed schoolkids might rule the roost during the day, this
beloved museum is for adults only when dusk falls. The monthly Lates
are something special: DJs entertain below the entrance hall's vast
blue whale skeleton, food and drink stalls pepper the corridors and
exhibitions – like the must-see Wildlife Photographer of the Year –
can be enjoyed without having to elbow people out the way.

## TATE MODERN

**Map 5; Bankside, Southwark; ///sparks.expert.thinks; www.tate.org.uk**

For gallery veterans marking the weekend and arts newbies looking
for some culture on a Friday night, Tate Modern's Uniqlo Lates have
become a popular fixture in the calendar. Taking place on the final
Friday of the month, these free events bring together and celebrate

creativity in all its forms, with banging tunes, challenging artworks and fun workshops. Of course, this is also the ideal opportunity to have a peek at the world-class modern art collection.

# V&A

### Map 4; Cromwell Road, South Kensington; ///boats.cards.hint; www.vam.ac.uk

Stylish, fashion-forward Londoners love the Victoria and Albert Museum. This design powerhouse has hosted sell-out exhibitions dedicated to wedding dresses, underwear and kimonos, plus creations by Christian Dior and Alexander McQueen. The free Lates, on the last Friday of the month, are a chance to delve behind the permanent displays, with visitors egged on to participate in performances, live installations and debates.

# NATIONAL GALLERY

### Map 1; Trafalgar Square, Charing Cross; ///rice.common.silver; www.nationalgallery.org.uk

This world-class collection opened in 1824 with the intention of bringing art to everybody. This ethos lives on now more than ever; it's free entry and there are daily talks covering everything from medieval portraiture to French Impressionism. Then there are the Friday night Lates, life-drawing classes, film screenings. Why shouldn't Van Gogh's *Sunflowers* brighten everybody's day?

**» Don't leave without** joining an Uncomfortable Art Tour, which aims to expose the role of colonial history in shaping collections.

# Solo, Pair, Crowd

**A day in London without a slice of culture is unthinkable, but there's always a way to get your fix.**

### FLYING SOLO
#### Walk and talk
Familiarize yourself with London's history, and make friends en route, on a Museum of London walking tour. Topics include the Great Fire of London and local queer history. Find out more online.

### IN A PAIR
#### Giggle with a date
Get past the first date awkwardness by joining a life-drawing class. The London Drawing Group offer pay-what-you-wish classes at the National Gallery.

### FOR A CROWD
#### Disco with dinosaurs
London's most unusual setting for a silent disco is the Natural History Museum's striking Hintz Hall. Here you and your mates can dance the night away under the suspended skeleton of Hope, the mascot blue whale.

## TATE BRITAIN

**Map 4; Millbank, Westminster; ///files.robe.native; www.tate.org.uk**

She might be overshadowed in popular opinion by her cool younger sister but, blimey, Tate Britain has a lot to offer. Like your art romantic? You'll love the Pre-Raphaelites. Prefer brighter paintings? Look out for David Hockney's works. Want to really immerse yourself in art? Check out the Late sessions, which are wonderfully community focused.

## BRITISH MUSEUM

**Map 1; Great Russell Street, Bloomsbury; ///unfair.purple.echo; www.britishmuseum.org**

The British Museum was the first national museum anywhere in the world to be open to the public and that spirit of inclusivity remains today, with free exhibitions every day of the week (as well as ticketed ones) and 20-minute spotlight tours on Fridays.

**» Don't leave without** checking out the controversial Parthenon Sculptures, which continue to spark debate about the legitimacy of removing cultural treasures from their homeland.

## SCIENCE MUSEUM

**Map 4; Exhibition Road, South Kensington; ///film.ozone.matter; www.sciencemuseum.org.uk**

On the last Wednesday of the month, the museum opens for adult-only, booze-friendly nights. Expect to get hands-on with science and ask all the big questions like "Could I survive an apocalypse?" and "Is my phone controlling my love life?"

# Indie Galleries

*This is a city that loves to push the boundaries,*
*especially when it comes to art. Paintings,*
*photography, installations: all are showcased*
*in the most weird and wonderful spaces.*

## THE CRYPT GALLERY

**Map 1; St Pancras Church, Euston; ///bids.crab.foil; www.cryptgallery.org**

In the early 1800s, departed Londoners were buried in church crypts rather than overcrowded graveyards. That was outlawed in 1854 – but the crypt at St Pancras Church had already interred 557 bodies. Their remains now watch over one of London's most atmospheric and macabre gallery spaces, where sound installations and art shows are erected among the underground stone alcoves and archways.

## 180 THE STRAND

**Map 1; 180 The Strand, Strand; ///opera.fairly.cloud;**
**www.180thestrand.com**

This Brutalist icon is home to one of London's most exciting creative centres. Having launched in 2016, the complex houses the likes of vinyl-pressing enterprise and record label The Vinyl Factory, alternative media group Dazed and music magazine *Fact*. These

While you're here, pop into Somerset House, which holds various exhibitions *(www. somersethouse.org.uk)*. creatives throw open their doors for some of the city's sexiest exhibitions, attracting art students and local office workers looking for a culture fix.

## THE PHOTOGRAPHERS' GALLERY

**Map 1; 16–18 Ramillies Street, Soho; ///forks.laptop.home; www.thephotographersgallery.org.uk**

Moved from various locations to this refitted old brick building, tucked behind Oxford Circus, this was the UK's first public gallery dedicated to the photographic arts – with a mission to promote the medium as one of our most significant artforms. As such, the classy space is a creative hub for all things photographic: exhibitions, yes, but also talks and events with London's art glitterati.

**» Don't leave without** visiting the bookshop, which stocks utterly gorgeous photography tomes – perfect for updating your coffee table.

## WHITE CUBE

**Map 5; 144–52 Bermondsey Street, Bermondsey; ///duty.scan.drum; www.whitecube.com**

In 1993, a tiny, square room in the art-dealing corner of the West End became a solo exhibition space with a rule that an artist could only be exhibited once. There many young British artists – such as Tracey Emin and Sarah Lucas – held career-changing shows. After an 11-year stint in Hoxton, the White Cube resides in Bermondsey and remains the go-to place for free-thinkers who worship conceptual art.

## SAATCHI GALLERY

**Map 4; Duke of York's HQ, King's Road, Chelsea; ///copy.boots.looked;**
**www.saatchigallery.com**

Much like the White Cube, this gallery became synonymous with young British artists in the 1990s, thanks to the promotion of talents like Hirst and Emin by Iraqi-British businessman Charles Saatchi. Today chic aficionados and wannabe art critics flock to the uber-cool Saatchi Gallery, keen to see the next big names in British art.

## THE OLD POLICE STATION

**Map 6; 114–16 Amersham Vale, New Cross; ///solid.renew.happy;**
**www.theoldpolicestation.org**

Have you ever been chin-stroking over an artwork and had to sidestep the toilet bowl that's blocking your view? This former police station-turned-gallery in New Cross might be the only place in the world where that's a real possibility. Ex-holding cells, busted open but with

Shh!

When wannabe hipsters pile off the carriage at Hackney Downs station, little do they know there is an indie gallery right there on platform 1. Banner Repeater is a contemporary and experimental art space, dedicated to developing art in a commuter station (*www. bannerrepeater.org*). You don't need to buy a ticket – though if you're disembarking be sure to tap out your payment card first, else you'll be charged a fine.

their latrines intact, have been converted into intimate exhibition spaces, while shipping containers outside house artist studios. The whole place has a DIY mindset, with artists collaborating on projects.

**>> Don't leave without** stopping in at Cartel, an adjoining contemporary art space based in a black shipping container.

## NOW GALLERY

**Map 6; Peninsula Square, Greenwich; ///admiral.hunt.handed; www.nowgallery.co.uk**

Looking to find the next big artist? Look no further. In the shadow of the Millennium Dome O2 Arena, this modern space is dedicated to representing a whole host of backgrounds and career levels in its art, fashion, photography and design shows. Two exhibitions return annually to promote young, diverse talent: Human Stories, a photographic series that unpicks social constructs around race and identity; and a Young Artist showcase to spotlight emerging talent.

## CAMDEN ART CENTRE

**Map 6; Arkwright Road, Hampstead; ///stem.slot.pies; www.camdenartcentre.org**

Not many tourists make it to Finchley Road, the busy stretch that extends from Regent's Park to Hampstead. But those that do are rewarded with this quiet and pleasant contemporary art space – a hidden gem that would draw much bigger crowds if they only knew it was here. The gallery also has a secret-garden café that draws local lunch-breakers craving its big slabs of quiche.

# Get Crafty

*Sometimes the best way to get to know a city, and the people who call it home, is to get hands on. Londoners love their crafts – whether handling cool clay, hot candle wax, just-cut blooms or neon pastels.*

## POTTERY AT THE KILN ROOMS

**Map 5; Unit 202 Level 2, Peckham town centre car park, 95A Rye Lane, Peckham; ///reform.smiled.likes; www.thekilnrooms.com**

Former multistorey car park Peckham Levels has been transformed into a hotbed for local talent, showcasing Peckham's small creative businesses. For the pottery-curious, the Kiln Rooms' five-hour taster sessions let you try your hand at clay work and create a few pieces of your own to be fire glazed. The perfect date activity (think *Ghost*).

### Try it!
### CRAFTIVISM

Keep an eye out for compassionate protests that use knitting and cross-stitching to convey anti-capitalist, environmental or feminist messages. Check out events with Craftivist Collective (*www.craftivist-collective.com*).

# THE FLOWER APPRECIATION SOCIETY

**Map 3; BE Studios, 72A Southgate Road, Hackney; ///harp.barks.tribe;**
**www.theflowerappreciationsociety.co.uk**

This floral studio hums with the chatter of girlfriends celebrating a birthday or bride-to-be. Run by two sisters who grow many of the blooms around the corner in an urban cutting garden, workshops cover everything from bridal bouquets to Christmas wreaths.

**» Don't leave without** buying a copy of A to Z of All Things Floral to keep crafty when you're back home.

# SOCIAL POTTERY

**Map 6; 120 Kentish Town Road, Kentish Town; ///fries.baking.press;**
**www.socialpottery.com**

There's something meditative about painting – less so when you've got all your mates around you and a gin tin in hand (it's BYO). Choose from hundreds of pottery pieces – mugs, jugs, bowls, pots – plus paints and stencils, and embrace your inner Picasso.

# MODERN CALLIGRAPHY AT VINTAGE HEAVEN

**Map 2; 82 Columbia Road, Hackney; ///foods.scarcely.shout;**
**www.alicegabb.com**

Been roped into writing your best friend's wedding invites? Lettering artist Alice Gabb is here to help with her calligraphy workshops. Alice supplies all the worksheets and words of wisdom you could possibly need, and the lovely folk of Vintage Heaven are on hand with cake.

## CLAY WORK SESSIONS AT KANA

**Map 3; 5A Gransden Avenue, London Fields; ///glass.flag.mason; www.kanalondon.com**

There's an individuality to Ana Kerin's handmade ceramics – the ghost of a subtle imperfection, the trace of a fingertip on the glaze, the echo of a hand across the surface. Tableware lovers should keep their eyes peeled for her workshops, where you can learn her hand-crafted, wheel-free style, with classes on everything from mug making to crafting your own crockery.

## LONDON TERRARIUMS

**Map 5; 106A New Cross Road, New Cross; ///couch.priced.delay; www.londonterrariums.com**

Londoners' unquenchable thirst for bringing greenery into their homes doesn't look set to slow down any time soon. For anyone who struggles to keep their plant babies alive, terrariums are the perfect low maintenance option. Check out terrarium making classes at London Terrariums, where you can craft your own self-contained tiny ecosystem of ferns, ivy and soft moss.

## CANDLEMAKING AT EARL OF EAST

**Map 3; 5 Gransden Avenue, Hackney; ///dock.tests.kite; www.earlofeast.com**

Warm Atlas cedar, the zing of Amalfi lemons, the faded smell of cigars that reminds you of your grandfather – scents can transport you to a place, person or memory. Crafting and preserving that nostalgic association in a candle is what the classes at Earl of East are all about. Learn to hand-pour your own soy wax candle in the magical scent lab before browsing the calming store, where class members get a 20 per cent discount.

## NEON NAKED LIFE DRAWING
**Map 2; 89 Great Eastern Street, Shoreditch; //assets.dinner.rival; www.neonnaked.com**

Art class meets Full Moon Party in this psychedelic life-drawing experience. Picture this: a dark room lit only by UV lights, a model glowing in reactive body paints, your neon pastels following their movements around the room. This is the activity for a sexy date night. Artist Jylle Navarro's background in fashion and performance inspired her to start these truly unique art classes, which take place at various locations across London, including in circus-inspired Trapeze Bar.

**>> Don't leave without** heading down into Trapeze Bar for a drink and acro-balance or contortion performance after your class.

Kintsugi is the latest Japanese craft to be quietly making itself known amongst Japanophiles and pottery lovers. Using gold resin to weld together cracks in treasured pieces of crockery, Kintsugi revolves around the idea that the mended product – with its now beautiful scars – is more precious than the original item. Check out Indytute for workshop listings *(www.indytute.com)*.

**Explore the glorious V&A**

This is the world's foremost art and design museum. Marvel at ancient ceramics, intricate wallpapers, and gorgeous theatre costumes.

BROMPTON ROAD

**4**

CROMWELL ROAD

THURLOE PLACE

BROMPTON ROAD

WALTON STREET

SOUTH KENSINGTON

OLD BROMPTON RD

*A celebration of French culture, the **Institut Français** on Queensbery Place opened its doors in 1908. Its Ciné Lumière draws film lovers today.*

**5**

**Dine at DAPHNE'S**

Devour delicious Italian fare – perhaps washed down with a glass of fizz – and admire the artworks that line the walls of this classy spot.

**3**

**Lunch at DOZO**

Restaurants don't get more stylish than Dozo. Grab a floor cushion, or *zabuton*, and order a Japanese bento box.

ONSLOW GARDENS

ROAD

FULHAM

SYDNEY

STREET

SLOANE AVE

CHELSEA

KING'S ROAD

OLD CHURCH STREET

*In 1964, fashion designer Mary Quant created the world's first-ever miniskirt in her boutique at **No. 138a King's Road**.*

KING'S ROAD

**2**

**Stock up on supplies at GREEN & STONE**

Feeling inspired? Buy everything you need to create your own masterpiece at this old and creaky art materials shop.

| 0 metres | 300 |
| --- | --- |
| 0 yards | 300 |

# A day ambling through
# arty West London

From its roots as an artists' colony in the 19th century to its heyday as the centre of the Swinging Sixties in the 20th, the borough of Kensington and Chelsea has long been an enviable postcode in the art world. An abundance of designer boutiques, paint shops and local galleries have drawn many notable residents to this area (think J M W Turner and Mick Jagger) and, today, cultural Kensington and swanky Chelsea remain stomping grounds for fashionistas, art collectors and eager-eyed designers.

BELGRAVIA

SLOANE STREET

SLOANE SQUARE

**1**

**Start at
SAATCHI GALLERY**
While away an hour or so at one of the world's most distinctive contemporary art centres before grabbing a coffee-to-go from the café.

**1. Saatchi Gallery**
King's Road, Chelsea;
www.saatchigallery.com;
///copy.boots.looked

**2. Green & Stone**
259 King's Road, Chelsea;
www.greenandstone.com;
///spine.woven.gloves

**3. Dozo**
68 Old Brompton Road,
South Kensington; www.
dozosushi.co.uk
///oasis.tops.actor

**4. V&A**
Cromwell Road, South
Kensington; www.vam.ac.uk;
///boats.cards.hint

**5. Daphne's**
112 Draycott Avenue,
Chelsea; www.daphnes-
restaurant.co.uk
///works.slim.gossip

**Institut Français**
///invite.raft.soccer

**138a Kings Road**
///tins.reach.lock

# NIGHTLIFE

*Whatever day of the week, London turns the volume up when darkness falls: groups descend on bustling food halls, musicians take to stages and revellers dance until dawn.*

# Evening Food Halls

*Something of a misnomer, these places aren't just about food. Animated crowds of friends line communal benches, bop to great tunes and charge their glasses. It's as much about socializing as sustenance.*

## MERCATO METROPOLITANO

**Map 5; 42 Newington Causeway, Elephant and Castle; ///people.rises.title; www.mercatometropolitano.com**

Elephant and Castle isn't the most happening place, we'll be honest, but it does have Mercato Metropolitano. You could pretty much live at this expansive street food mecca, which is open all day every day but comes into its own in the evening. As dusk falls, the leafy courtyards and vast rooms of food stalls and bars fill out with a diverse crowd of

### Try it!
### COOK ITALIAN

Mercato Metropolitano is all about sustainability and community – as well as good food. Meet the skilled Mercato chefs at a zero-waste pasta-making class. Profits go to London charities, too.

good-timers chatting over chewy-crusted pizzas and steaming bowls of ramen. There are always plenty of seats and it never feels over-crowded – perfect for raucous evenings with all your loved ones.

## FLAT IRON SQUARE

**Map 5; 68 Union Street, Bermondsey; ///gone.heave.almost; www.flatironsquare.co.uk**

Six cavernous railway arches, a festoon-light-draped courtyard and a Georgian townhouse have combined into an eating, drinking and entertainment hub, open Wednesday through Sunday. After-work chitchat and lively music form a buzzing soundtrack, smoky scents lure punters into the food-trader-lined archways, and craft beer is knocked back ahead of gigs in the Omeara music venue.

**>> Don't leave without** sneaking off to the Tap & Bottle, Flat Iron Square's intimate, little-known wine bar and secluded roof terrace.

## MODEL MARKET

**Map 6; 196 Lewisham High Street, Lewisham; ///plans.parade.slower; www.streetfeast.com**

Lucky it's open till 1am (Fridays and Saturdays) as you could easily spend a whole night here. It's a place to head en masse – bring your mates, and their mates, and make some new mates while you're here too – such is the party atmosphere. Yep, it's next to a tired-looking shopping centre but looks aren't everything. Expect to find a buzzing tequila bar, thumping soundtrack and treats from London street food royalty, like Fundi Pizza.

# BOXPARK

**Map 2; 2–10 Bethnal Green Road, Shoreditch; ///drip.ballots.flank; www.boxpark.co.uk**

Boxpark might be London's definitive pop-up market. Set in shipping containers opposite Shoreditch High Street train station, it's home to some of the city's best street food (don't miss the vegan eats from What the Pitta). This is the place to be seen; cool kids sip cocktails, snap photos and enjoy the beats spun by up-and-coming DJ talent, grime MCs and soulful house DJs.

# MARE STREET MARKET

**Map 3; 115 Mare Street, Hackney; ///donor.hobby.they; www.marestreetmarket.com**

Anything Shoreditch can do, Hackney can do better. Just look at Mare Street Market, a former job centre that has been transformed into an indoor food hall with a strict no-plastic policy. It's open every day of the week but it's especially buzzy on weekends, when trendy millennials decked out in athleisure wear descend in their droves to browse the market's delis and quaff locally brewed beers.

# POP BRIXTON

**Map 5; 49 Brixton Station Road, Brixton; ///bridge.beyond.lamps; www.popbrixton.org**

Vibey, loud and always packed, Pop Brixton is Brixton's go-to destination for foodie, boozy alfresco nights out. Two levels of colour-splashed shipping containers — dens for tiny eateries and

Pop Brixton too much? Try Brixton Village and Market Row – you'll get a seat and won't have to shout.

bars – are packed with a young crowd, beers in hand, every night of the week. Music thumps in the background and the scent of fried food fills the air.

## TOOTING MARKET

### Map 6; 21–3 Tooting High Street, Tooting; ///shells.labs.straw; www.tootingmarket.com

For too long Brixton has held the limelight. Enter Tooting, a foodie's paradise with a lovely community feel. Come evening and Tooting Market is a hive of activity: families devour bowls of bubbling curry, students discuss politics over steaming ramen and professionals clink wine glasses. The market also has a cool younger sister, Tooting Broadway Market, just a short hop away.

>> **Don't leave without** one last drink at Tap 13, a zero-waste tap bar with a great atmosphere in Tooting Broadway Market.

## EATALY

### Map 2; 135 Bishopsgate, Liverpool Street; ///maple.flies.field; www.eataly.co.uk

City slickers rejoiced when Eataly threw open its doors in 2021, descending on the Liverpool Street food market to get their fill of *bellissimo* Italian fare and glasses of prosecco. And who can blame them? Replete with various restaurants, food stalls, a drinking terrace and even a cookery school, there's something to keep you busy and, more imporantly, well-fed every night of the week.

# Game Night

*Millennials are getting married and buying flats but the thought of growing old brings them out in hives. Luckily there's plenty of places to put their maturity aside and revel in a bit of friendly competition.*

## FLIGHT CLUB

### Map 1; 55 New Oxford Street, Bloomsbury; ///crafty.study.judge; www.flightclubdarts.com

The humble game of darts has been drawn out of the shadows of old-school boozers and given a high-energy makeover. Everything about this place is fun: the noughties tunes, the tear-and-share pizza and, of course, the darts games themselves. Flight Club is perfect for a group activity, whether you're looking for genuinely enjoyable team bonding or weekend tomfoolery with your London family.

## FOUR QUARTERS

### Map 5; 187 Rye Lane, Peckham; ///codes.unwanted.modest; www.geocities.fourquartersbar.co.uk

Packed-out with retro consoles and arcade games, and set to the soundtrack of concentrated thumb tapping, this is where South London's hipsters come for a bout of gaming nostalgia. Evenings

After a red-eyed night at Four Quarters, refuel at Mr Bao, Peckham's popular Taiwanese restaurant. | are frittered away going square-eyed on Pac Man or battling it out in an intense gaming tournament. Whoever loses buys the next round of beers.

# THE CRYSTAL MAZE LIVE EXPERIENCE

**Map 1; 22–32 Shaftesbury Avenue, Piccadilly; ///oldest.likes.super; www.the-crystal-maze.com**

We salute the wacky team that decided to resurrect 1990s game show *The Crystal Maze* in real life. The immersive game of mental, physical and skilfull challenges is overseen by an entertaining Maze Master, making for a very memorable birthday, hen or stag do. Tickets aren't cheap and it books up far in advance – but trust us, it's just about the most fun you will ever have.

**» Don't leave without** getting a photo in your iconic satin bomber jacket – you can even buy one to take home.

# BALLIE BALLERSON

**Map 2; 97–113 Curtain Road, Shoreditch; ///beard.minds.keen; www.ballieballerson.com**

Remember the pure, unadulterated joy of launching yourself into a ball pit? Relive those childhood memories at this Shoreditch playground for grown-ups, which features two ball pits and a ball pit waterfall. The excited shrieks of 20-somethings clowning around in the pits are accompanied by a banging soundtrack of R'n'B and disco beats. It makes for a night to remember.

## ALL STAR LANES

**Map 1; Victoria House, Bloomsbury Place, Holborn; ///worry.drew.duty;**
**www.allstarlanes.co.uk**

Relive the fun-filled birthdays of your childhood with an evening of
bowling – this time washed down with beers and cocktails. Popular
with groups of over-excited office workers looking to unwind after
work, All Star Lanes even has a number of karaoke booths so you
can make a proper night of it.

## ROOF EAST

**Map 6; Stratford multistorey car park, Great Eastern Way, Stratford;**
**///grades.translated.tower; www.roofeast.com**

This place taps into not one but two of London's weaknesses – an
insatiable thirst for rooftop bars and an obsession with transforming
car parks into fun spaces. As soon as summer hits, grown-up

**Shh!**

Ever played Cluedo on a
London red bus? No, we thought
not, and you're not alone – not
many Londoners have
discovered this gem. Wood
Green's double-decker café
Cakes and Ladders has more
than 500 board games for you
to play inside, or in its outdoor
space *(www.cakesandladders.
co.uk)*. The menu is all locally
sourced too, so you can feel
smug about tucking into one
of its famous Wilde's Cheese
toasties while playing Monopoly
with your favourite people.

city-dwellers scale the heights of Roof East to run riot at this playground. Dating duos flirt their way around the crazy golf, while mates battle it out in the batting cages – all fuelled by the ubiquitous craft beer and street food, of course.

## THE ARCH CLIMBING WALL

**Map 5; 100 Clements Road, Bermondsey; ///risk.fork.press; www.archclimbingwall.com**

Decent climbing walls are easy to come by in the capital these days but it's hard to beat this Bermondsey site. Natural lighting meets an extensive range of walls for nervy beginners right through to pro boulderers competing for the highest vantage point. Whatever your level, expert climbers are always happy to dish out tips. Once you're all climbed out, toast yourself at the breweries on Bermondsey Beer Mile.

## JUNKYARD GOLF CLUB

**Map 2; 88 Worship Street, Hackney; ///toward.lonely.grapes; www.junkyardgolfclub.co.uk**

You wouldn't expect a weird and wonderful nine-hole golf course made from scrapyard slides and disused car parts to work, but it does. Especially with its array of cocktails served in red party cups and garnished with bonbons and Jammy Dodger biscuits. Junkyard Golf is pure, unadulterated fun for big kids, so book in your mates and get putting to the beats of old-school hip hop.

**» Don't leave without** buying a bag of pick-n-mix; you'll get flashbacks to carefully choosing penny sweets in the corner shop as a kid.

# Live Music

*The Rolling Stones, Coldplay, Florence and the Machine, Dizzee Rascal – these music gods all started their careers here in London. And the city's venues continue to host incredible acts across all genres.*

## ROUNDHOUSE

### Map 1; Chalk Farm Road, Camden Town; ///swear.relate.pushes; www.roundhouse.org.uk

Most Londoners will have heard of the Roundhouse, fewer will know why it's round: its circular shape dates back to when it was a railway engine repair shed. These days, it's one of London's most sacred venues and a beloved Camden landmark. Theatre, spoken word and circus shows are performed here but it's live music that lures young rockers and indie lovers in their droves.

## THE HAGGERSTON

### Map 3; 438 Kingsland Road, Dalston; ///bugs.loyal.early; 020 7923 3206

A topsy-turvy pub with a ramshackle back garden, this icon is remembered by longtime East Enders as Uncle Sam's, where Sunday-night jazz sessions would keep the party going until 3am. The management changed hands in 2008 but the jazz remained,

Sate your appetite before (or after) the jazz at Chick'n'Sours, just next door. The chicken tenders are the perfect pick-me-up.

and it's still the safest bet for a memorable Sunday night out in East London. It can get rammed – the *feng shui* needs work – but the musical talent is rock solid, matched by a trendy, friendly crowd.

## UNION CHAPEL

### Map 6; 19B Compton Terrace, Islington; ///number.tribe.author; www.unionchapel.org.uk

How often have you cradled a cup of tea while watching a gig? A far cry from the booze-fuelled, jostling floors of many venues, the Union Chapel is a magical experience. Set in a Grade I-listed Gothic masterpiece, this is a calm space where a spellbound audience fills church pews. With its soaring acoustics and ornate stained-glass window forming a glowing backdrop, it's perfect for stripped-back gigs.

## JAZZ CAFE

### Map 1; 5 Parkway, Camden Town; ///nodded.jolly.hulk; www.thejazzcafelondon.com

In 2020 the Jazz Cafe celebrated 30 years as London's temple to hip hop, jazz, funk and soul, with royalty like Erykah Badu, D'Angelo, Amy Winehouse and The Pharcyde having all graced its stage. The 440-capacity venue hosts DJs and MCs for weekend shows, with cool Londoners busting serious moves to their beats.

>> **Don't leave without** checking out the upstairs balcony, where you can book a dinner table with an uninterrupted view of the musicians.

# EARTH (EVOLUTIONARY ARTS HACKNEY)

**Map 3; 11–17 Stoke Newington Road, Dalston; ///demand.fool.humble; www.earthackney.co.uk**

Hackney residents were gutted when, in 2018, the iconically down-and-out Efes Snooker Club put down its cues for the last time. But in the building's place came EartH: a multi-arts venue with a community-focused ethos and a line-up of new rap and jazz talent.

**» Don't leave without** pausing for a drink and a cultural chat with the locals on the first floor's secret garden terrace.

# HOOTANANNY

**Map 5; 95 Effra Road, Brixton; ///life.bake.insect; www.hootannanybrixton.co.uk**

A hootananny isn't just what Jools Holland gets up to on New Year's Eve; Brixton pub Hootananny is all about letting your hair down and savouring great live music. It's one of London's premier places to spot up-and-coming musicians of a head-spinningly diverse range of genres, and to dance yourself into a glowing, ecstatic frenzy.

# OMEARA

**Map 5; 6 O'Meara Street, London Bridge; ///mixed.prefer.sketch; www.omearalondon.com**

In an exposed-brick archway, this live music venue is owned by Mumford & Sons' Ben Lovett – but its gig offerings go way beyond the banjo-twanging folk rock that the London band is famed for.

Omeara has steadily become one of London's top places to headhunt brand-new rap and grime artists, among many other genres. And come the weekend the music venue escalates into a nightclub, with a second bar room transforming into a dance floor and DJs bringing the house and funk.

## VILLAGE UNDERGROUND
### Map 2; 54 Holywell Lane, Shoreditch; ///jelly.rust.pens;
### www.villageunderground.co.uk

Music-loving Londoners know that pulse-quickening moment when they get tickets to a gig at Village Underground. Why? Well, music venues don't get much cooler. Tucked behind a nondescript door, this expansive venue is strong on atmosphere, thanks to its cavernous roof, gloomy archways and industrial warehouse vibe. Apparently 1,000 gig-goers can fit in here but it never feels that way – it's a space that creates a magnetic sense of intimacy despite its size. Expect new talent and a crowd of (sweaty) ravers.

Shoreditch's Troy Bar *(www. troybar.co.uk)* bills itself as London's best-kept secret. One night spent bopping along to live funk jams or reggae acts, or daring to participate in Tuesdays' open mic nights will leave you with a serious dilemma: to shout it from the rooftops, or keep the secret to yourself? Either way, you'll be making a return visit.

# Culture Live

*Sure, the West End has its place but the real drama is found in the city's indie theatres and performance spaces. Dance, drag, burlesque, comedy – whatever you're into, London's got it.*

## WILTON'S MUSIC HALL

**Map 2; 1 Graces Alley, Whitechapel; ///bottom.prompting.fish; www.wiltons.org.uk**

Fancy a night of swinging mischief with an all-female cabaret band? Or one-man show "The One With Gunther", which retells the entirety of *Friends* in an hour? Join a kooky crowd and immerse yourself in fringe theatre at Wilton's, the world's oldest surviving music hall.

**» Don't leave without** having a drink at the Mahogony Bar, which was built back in 1826 and was later used as a soup kitchen during the Blitz.

## BARBICAN CENTRE

**Map 2; Silk Street, Barbican; ///forces.rubble.lake; www.barbican.org.uk**

Don't be fooled by the stark 1980s exterior; the Barbican is a cultural powerhouse. Home of the London Symphony Orchestra and Royal Shakespeare Company, here you'll also discover curious art exhibitions, indie cinema screenings and electric live performances.

## SADLER'S WELLS

**Map 1; Rosebery Avenue, Angel; ///hints.square.tracks;**
**www.sadlerswells.com**

Dance lovers know there's no beating Sadler's Wells, London's dedicated home for contemporary dance with over three centuries' worth of theatrical heritage. A stripped-back, unfussy space, here you'll find an accessible programme of dance in all forms: loosened-up ballet, Bollywood, fiery flamenco, street dance and bags more besides.

## THE BILL MURRAY

**Map 2; 39 Queens Head Street, Angel; ///quiz.feeds.rash;**
**www.angelcomedy.co.uk**

There's no mistaking which London pub is dedicated to comedy: the mural of Charlie Chaplin is a giveaway. Once a shabby pub, the Bill Murray was taken over by Angel Comedy Club, which also hosts stand-up nights at the Camden Head down the road. There's a free show every night, so it's always busy with Londoners looking for a laugh. Cross your fingers for a celeb comic trying out new material.

### Try it!
### STAND-UP COMEDY

Got a notebook filled with jokes that you've been waiting to try on an audience? Email raw@angelcomedy.co.uk as far in advance as you can and test your mettle on one of the most welcoming comedy stages in town.

# Solo, Pair, Crowd

**A night to yourself? Struggling for date night ideas? Craving a night out with the gang? London's cultural scene has got something for every occasion.**

## SOLO
### Cheap theatre for one
Bag £10 preview ticket for a show at The Old Vic, a world-leading, independent, not-for-profit theatre near the South Bank. They go on sale around five weeks in advance, so keep an eye on the website.

## IN A PAIR
### Cuddle up at an intimate gig
Founded in a London living room, Sofar Sounds now hosts gigs with unknowns in unusual places across the city. You might get a jazz band, a spoken-word artist or a classical flautist. Just bring beer and blankets.

## IN A CROWD
### Watch musical legends with the crew
Get tickets for a gig at Camden's glorious Roundhouse *(p144)*. You can't beat the feeling of rocking out with all your pals around you.

## GIN HOUSE BURLESQUE

**Map 2; King's Head, 257 Kingsland Road, Haggerston;**
**///ripe.buzz.judges; www.ginhouseburlesque.com**

Push through the scraggy doors of the old King's Head pub for
good-humoured bawdiness at Gin House Burlesque. Don't expect
a classy night, rather burlesque teases, saucy drag queens and
rowdy sing-alongs amid a menagerie of taxidermy.

## SOUTHBANK CENTRE

**Map 5; Belvedere Road, South Bank; ///alien.cave.discouraged;**
**www.southbankcentre.co.uk**

A vast, Brutalist concrete slab on the banks of the Thames, the
Southbank Centre is loved by Londoners. The backdrop for after-
work drinks, it also happens to be one of the city's best cultural hubs
with its three venues showcasing gigs, theatre, debates and more.

## BETHNAL GREEN
## WORKING MEN'S CLUB

**Map 2; 42–4 Pollard Row, Bethnal Green; ///angle.epic.elaborate;**
**www.workersplaytime.net**

Mischief is key to a night at this former working men's club, which has
been hosting socials since 1887. Bring your entourage and get ready
to slay with a glorious cast of alternative queens and performers. It's
about as inclusive, quirky and raucous as an East London night can be.

**» Don't leave without** heading downstairs to the cosy Workers Arms
for a quick pint and game of Jenga with a more sedate crowd.

# Cool Clubs

*Clubbing in London is a world-class experience. Top-tier DJs keep movers and shakers dancing every night of the week, with line-ups easily competing with some of the world's most famous superclubs.*

## PECKHAM AUDIO

### Map 5; 133A Rye Lane, Peckham; ///lifts.curving.rice; www.peckhamaudio.co.uk

After a hard week at work, the city's coolest chuck on their favourite trainers and make for a night out in Peckham. Some of South London's best nightlife outfits are found along Rye Lane, not least subterranean Peckham Audio. This exclusive venue has quietly made a name for itself on the alternative clubbing circuit thanks to its top-of-the-range sound system and top-notch house and techno producers.

## XOYO

### Map 2; 32–7 Cowper Street, Shoreditch; ///quest.bath.soup; www.xoyo.co.uk

It's no exaggeration to say that London's best electronic line-ups are found at this underground Shoreditch staple. XOYO's programme favours quality music and genres span house, techno, drum and bass, grime and hip hop. DJ residencies are world-class – Palms Trax, Andy C, Calibre to name a few – and keep London's party people dancing into the early hours of the morning.

**»** **Don't leave without** swinging by the Banksy graffiti, hidden behind a kebab shop around the corner (where Old Street meets Great Eastern).

# PRINTWORKS

### Map 5; Surrey Quays, Canada Water; ///today.wiring.eagle; www.printworkslondon.co.uk

The transformation of a vast former printing press into this music and culture space was big clubbing news back in 2017 and the hype hasn't ended. At a capacity of 3,000, and with headline acts performing in a huge laser-lit hall that's as high-ceilinged as it is long, this daytime clubbing experience is epic in all respects. Though be warned: there are long queues for the bar, for the toilets, and to actually get in in the first place. It's worth it though.

# FOLD

### Map 6; Gillian House, Canning Town; ///flight.passes.state; www.residentadvisor.net

Not long after Printworks found its stride, this 600-capacity ravers' dream opened its doors with a hedonistic electro programme. Its industrial setting is in the middle of nowhere (though rest assured there's a Tube station within a 10-minute walk) so party nights feel private. Be ready to dance with abandon alongside clubbers whose spirits hark back to the 1990s warehouse days.

## TOOTING TRAM & SOCIAL

**Map 6; 46–8 Mitcham Road, Tooting; ///intend.churn.types;**
**www.tootingtramandsocial.co.uk**

It may not look much from the outside but this cavernous converted
tram shed promises a great night. A casual hangout in the day,
come evening the table football and time-worn chesterfield sofas
are pushed aside as a fun and friendly crowd of young professionals
dance to hip hop and R'n'B classics.

## BRIXTON JAMM

**Map 5; 261 Brixton Road, Brixton; ///spots.stow.pest; www.brixtonjamm.org**

Brixton Jamm is a shapeshifter. A favoured student haunt and the
site of many community-focused events, the versatile venue is also
a favoured after-party spot for O2 Academy gig-goers. Here you'll

If you're in the market for
a proper locals' clubbing
experience, scope out
Mick's Garage, a renovated
warehouse in Hackney Wick.
In collaboration with the
next-door brewery CRATE,
the multipurpose events space
hosts pop-up coffee and street
food in the daytime, and DJ
sets held by party throwers
Flamingo Pier and Whirl-y-Gig
at night. Mick's Garage is a
regular for the coolest of the
cool and, if you meet the right
people, you might even get an
invite to another exclusive
warehouse party nearby.

find disco day parties on its huge terrace, sweaty grime sessions in its (thankfully air-conditioned) main room and actor and DJ Craig Charles's legendary Funk and Soul Club.

## RIDLEY ROAD MARKET BAR

**Map 3; 49 Ridley Road, Dalston; ///item.forgot.farm;**
**www.ridleyroadmarketbar.com**

This scruffbag spot masks its office-like panelled ceilings and sticky floors with tropical décor in its bid for a tiki beach bar vibe. The drinks are mercifully cheap, with tins of Red Stripe at £3, cocktails £5. And the beats of Motown and reggae keeps a down-to-earth crowd dancing until the lights are turned up in the early hours. Leave your pretentions at the door (and start queuing for the toilet 15 minutes in advance).

**» Don't leave without** enjoying a 10-inch, £5 pizza from Slice Girls, self-named "90s babes" who have been feeding partygoers since 2013.

## DALSTON SUPERSTORE

**Map 3; 117 Kingsland High Street, Dalston; ///remove.brief.heads;**
**www.dalstonsuperstore.com**

Indie LGBTQ+ venues are under threat in London, falling victim to the city's rising rents and property development. This fact makes the community vibe and consistently full dance floor at Superstore feel even more special. Londoners flock here for the club's fondness for drag queens dancing on the bar, the queer art displayed all over the walls, and the club's wonderful ability to segue from sickly sweet pop upstairs to dark, techno filth in the basement.

# LGBTQ+ Scene

*London is globally recognized as an LGBTQ+ capital,
thanks to its vibrant queer history and fabulous
nightlife scene. You'll be welcomed with open arms
at a number of inclusive venues and theatre spots.*

## THE GLORY

**Map 2; 281 Kingsland Road, Haggerston; ///stale.pill.cared; www.theglory.co**
Drag queen superstar Jonny Woo teamed up with drag DJ John Sizzle
to launch this performance powerhouse and party pub. It's become
big on the scene since its 2015 opening, thanks to its glittering stage
hosting a whole lotta drag. In daylight hours, The Glory holds talks
about the history of gay life in Hackney; come nightfall, things get
steamy in the basement, when a young, alternative crowd hit the floor.

## ROYAL VAUXHALL TAVERN

**Map 5; 372 Kennington Lane, Vauxhall; ///master.plank.stable;
www.vauxhalltavern.com**
It's said that after a nuclear holocaust all that would be left are
cockroaches, Cher and the Royal Vauxhall Tavern. This legendary
Grade II-listed performance venue dates back to 1863 but it left
its Victorian sensibilities behind many moons ago. The RVT has

played a key role in London's and, more specifically, Vauxhall's gay history. And the community love it, so much so that they've campaigned to protect the tavern from property developers countless times. No trip to central London is complete without popping into this sacred place.

**»** **Don't leave without** upping the ante at Fire, just around the corner. It's a great way to complete your experience of gay nightlife in Vauxhall.

## ABOVE THE STAG THEATRE

**Map 5; 72 Albert Embankment, Vauxhall; ///menu.loudly.rises; www.abovethestag.org.uk**

Another Vauxhall stalwart, Above the Stag is the UK's only full-time, professional LGBTQ+ theatre. It has one fundamental aim: to use storytelling to give an elevated voice to the community. To that end, musicals, plays, readings, comedy and more all have their turn in the limelight here. Come December, the theatre hosts the one Christmas pantomime it's definitely worth donning your festive knit for; get tickets for you and your squad and prepare for a night to remember.

## SHE SOHO

**Map 1; 23A Old Compton Street, Soho; ///scales.racing.thing; www.ku-bar.co.uk**

London's only exclusively queer women's venue is all about having a good time with lively DJ sets and top-drawer drag king peformances. Though mainly catering to women, everyone is welcome; the organizers just want people to party hard in a safe space.

## Liked by the locals

**"London's gay scene is a veritable treasure trove. Sip on champagne and cocktails with the immaculately coiffed Soho boys in trendy Ku Bar, then dance the weekend away at G-A-Y Late, the only place in central London open until 3am on a Sunday."**

PATRICK CASH, FOUNDER OF SPOKEN WORD LONDON

## ADONIS AT THE CAUSE

**Map 6; Ashley House, Ashley Road, Tottenham; ///over.hails.remove; www.supportthecause.co.uk**

Nights out don't get more in-your-face than this. Expect risqué outfits, delicious debauchery and thumping techno as a mob of young ravers live their best lives. The grass-roots venue also organizes other events focused on inclusion and mental health in the LGBTQ+ community, which creates a wonderfully friendly feeling.

## BIG DYKE ENERGY

**Map 5; Unit 18, Surrey Canal Road, Bermondsey; ///quiz.boost.events**

The clue is in the name: this place is all about the empowerment of queer women. Anything goes in this no-rules club: dress up or dress down. Hit the floor with no inhibitions or stick to the bar. Bring your friends or come alone. No matter what, you'll feel the joy of the party.

## THE KARAOKE HOLE

**Map 3; 95 Kingsland High Street, Dalston; ///breath.drive.haven; www.thekaraokehole.com**

The owners of Dalston Superstore blessed Londoners with a genius concept: karaoke led by the city's finest drag stars. A fabulous host will encourage and mock you through your rendition of "Total Eclipse of the Heart". Want more? Wait for the arrival of queer Usher impersonator Gusher, or divine intervention from Shesus.

**»  Don't leave without** grabbing an enormous slice of pizza from Voodoo Ray's, upstairs from the Karaoke Hole.

## SHACKLEWELL LANE

### 1 A bite to eat at DEL74

Chow down on tacos and quesadillas while bopping to retro tunes at this jolly haunt.

*The indie* **Rio Cinema** *has been screening films since 1915 but, in the 70s, it briefly staged live burlesque and striptease acts.*

SANDRINGHAM ROAD

KINGSLAND HIGH ST

### Grab the mic at 2 THE KARAOKE HOLE

A cohort of drag queens host nights at this underground spot. Prepare your best Madonna impersonation for a karaoke experience like no other.

**Ridley Road** *might be quiet at night but during the day it's a busy marketplace – a scene that's little changed since the 1880s.*

BRADBURY STREET

KINGSLAND HIGH STREET

RIDLEY ROAD

BOLEYN ROAD

**DALSTON**

### 3 A quick game at DRAUGHTS

Need a breather? Head to this low-key board game bar for a glass of wine and game of Jenga or Hungry Hippos.

| 0 metres | 100 |
| 0 yards | 100 |

## An evening in
# Dalston's dive bars

The secret's out: Dalston is where it's at. People flock here from all over town (and farther afield) to be seen in the neighbourhood's basement bars, vegan restaurants and backstreet pubs. Rising rents have seen the end of some beloved grassroots nightlife spots, but Dalston is still one of London's most vibrant and multicultural areas. You can't get to know East London without spending a night trawling Kingsland High Street, ideally after an afternoon shopping in its indie boutiques and charity shops.

**1. Del74**
129 Kingsland High
Street, Dalston;
www.tacosdel74.com;
///guards.finely.update

**2. The Karaoke Hole**
95 Kingsland High
Street, Dalston;
www.thekaraokehole.com;
///truck.cool.tens

**3. Draughts**
41 Kingsland High
Street, Dalston;
www.draughtslondon.com;
///privately.occurs.tubes

**4. Ridley Road Market Bar**
49 Ridley Road, Dalston;
www.ridleyroadmarket
bar.com;
///item.forgot.farm

COLVESTONE CRESCENT

**4**

**Dance at
RIDLEY ROAD
MARKET BAR**
End the night's proceedings at this tropical-themed locals' spot, where the beers are cheap and the tunes are banging.

**Rio Cinema** ///dimes.copies.during

# OUTDOORS

*It might be a metropolis but London isn't lacking on the outdoors front. Come rain or shine, locals love nothing more than a walk in the park or a dip in an open-air lido.*

# Swimming Spots

*As far as a Londoner is concerned, anything above 24°C is summer. With sunglasses on and swimmers at the ready, it's straight to a lido, where it's as much about being seen as it is actually swimming.*

## SERPENTINE LIDO

**Map 4; Hyde Park, Kensington; ///starts.buzz.popped;**
**www.royalparks.org.uk**

Come summer and Hyde Park's resident swans are forced to share this lido with the masses. Sun-worshippers pepper the grounds around the water, rowers glide just beyond the swimming barrier and mates enjoy a splash around. Things are quieter for the swans in winter, though the hardy members of the Serpentine Swimming Club – Britain's oldest of its kind – insist upon plunging into the chilly depths each morning.

## LONDON FIELDS LIDO

**Map 3; London Fields West Side, Hackney; ///unit.learns.river;**
**020 7254 9038**

You'll be pleased to hear that London Fields' Olympic-sized pool is heated so whatever the weather you're in for a pleasant dip. And you'll really enjoy the buzzy community vibes, too. Young Hackney parents dip their babies in the water here and friends compete over who can swim the most lengths, before hardcore swimmers arrive for a peaceful nighttime swim beneath the lido's flapping bunting.

» **Don't leave without** a pick-me-up coffee and falafel wrap from the café. Enjoy on the terrace while watching your fellow swimmers.

## BROCKWELL LIDO

**Map 5; Brockwell Park, Dulwich Road, Brixton; ///petal.broom.open; www.brockwelllido.com**

Set on the fringes of Brockwell Park, this outdoor pool is a beloved landmark – so much so that you can even get married here. The Grade II-listed Art Deco building that surrounds the waters makes for an attractive backdrop (it also houses the popular Lido Café, which does a knockout brunch). The pool is unheated so it's one for the hardy swimmers among you – though when a heatwave hits, the lido is suddenly at the forefront of everyone's minds.

## CHARLTON LIDO

**Map 6; Hornfair Park, Shooters Hill Road, Greenwich; ///haven.curvy.chin; 020 8856 7389**

Charlton Lido's claims to fame include starring in a Blazin' Squad music video in 2003 and an episode of police drama *The Bill* in 2004. Such dizzying heights aside, the 1930s lido underwent a £2 million facelift in 2013 and now it has it all: two sun terraces, a gym, and a state-of-the-art fitness studio, plus a fully heated pool. Bring your own squad and enjoy a dip; it's open all year round.

# HAMPSTEAD HEATH PONDS

**Map 6; Hampstead Heath, Hampstead; ///jobs.crown.ranged;**
**www.hampsteadheath.net**

A community of thick-skinned regulars swim here through the winter. For mere mortals, it's the first signs of summer that put the heath's Mixed Pond and its segregated alternatives on the map. Yes, the waters are murky and ducks bob about on the surface, but going wild swimming here is the best escape from the city.

**>> Don't leave without** giving a donation at whichever pond you take a dip in. In doing so you'll be supporting the wonderful lifeguards.

# PARLIAMENT HILL LIDO

**Map 6; Heath Lodge, Highgate; ///money.added.goes;**
**www.parliamenthilllido.org**

Don't fancy sharing your swim with the local wildlife of Hampstead? Then head to the heath's other dipping option, the Parliament Hill Lido. It's a few degrees warmer and altogether more refined than its neighbour. There's also a toasty sauna, perfect for drying off.

# TOOTING BEC LIDO

**Map 6; Tooting Bec Road, Tooting; ///case.badge.raced; www.slsc.org.uk**

This is the largest outdoor freshwater pool in the UK and arguably London's most popular lido. When school's out for summer, excited kids and their weary parents head to Tooting Bec Lido to splash about in its waters. Meanwhile groups of friends line the concrete to chat, people-watch and top up their vitamin D before taking a cooling dip.

## Liked by the locals

"The ponds don't feel like London. I love going first thing, when it's freezing and misty. Everyone's bonded by the cold – shivering but smiling. And you can tell who the hardcore swimmers are by their sensible woolly hats."

NESS WHEELER, YOGA TEACHER, FILM PRODUCER AND REGULAR SWIMMER AT HAMPSTEAD HEATH LADIES' POND

# Green Spaces

*This is the world's first National Park City, didn't you know? Londoners are very proud of this fact, and rightly so. After all, there are countless parks, rich with wildlife, sitting right on their doorstep.*

## RICHMOND PARK

### Map 6; entrance via Richmond Gate, Richmond; ///barks.vine.fees; www.royalparks.org.uk

Some Londoners might say that Richmond isn't *really* in London, it being so far out, but that would be denying the city its greatest slice of wilderness. A rambling expanse of tousled meadows, dappled woodland and reed-fringed ponds, this is where city-dwellers go to let off steam and get closer to nature. Things are quieter on weekdays,

### Try it!
### PHOTOGRAPH NATURE

Extend your time in leafy Richmond with a trip to Kew Gardens, a botanical masterpiece. Here you can join photography classes with specialist tree and forest photographer Edward Parker.

when roaming herds of deer rule the park, but come the weekend it's a hive of activity – dog-walkers stop to make conversation, cyclists tackle the muddy tracks and groups walk off their Sunday roasts.

# HAMPSTEAD HEATH

**Map 6; entrance via South End Road, Hampstead; ///fakes.prime.album; www.hampsteadheath.net**

Just a couple of stops on the underground from gritty Camden is Hampstead Heath, the wild, undulating lungs of North London. You could spend days rambling across the heath's acres of parkland and foraging in its fruitful meadows, not forgetting dipping a toe in one of its willowy ponds (p166). However long you're here, a walk up to Parliament Hill for its spectacular views of the London skyline is essential, especially followed by a pint at the Spaniards Inn (p76).

**» Don't leave without** wandering through the plant-entangled Hampstead Hill Gardens and Pergola – it's elegant and eerie all at once.

# VICTORIA PARK

**Map 3; entrance via Crown Gate East, Bow; ///poppy.hears.deny**

Families hot-foot it to the boating lake, friends play rounders on the lawn, joggers thud along the running track; this green space lives up to its moniker of the "People's Park", so given in Victorian times because it was intended for the use of ordinary East Enders. In the summer, when festivals aren't on, Vicky Park (another affectionate nickname) is the place to come armed with a bottle of plonk and fresh supplies from nearby Victoria Park Village's delis and bakeries.

# LONDON FIELDS

**Map 3; entrance on Lansdowne Drive, Hackney; ///clever.zips.fills**

There's a lovely village feel about London Fields, thanks in part to its proximity to independent-led Broadway Market *(p104)*. Old boys read the paper on park benches, looking up to watch families cycling along the park's paths. Hipsters sprawled across the grass, coffees in hand, put the world to rights. Competitive couples battle it out at the communal ping pong table. This is the place to while away a Saturday.

# BROCKWELL PARK

**Map 5; entrance via Brixton Water Lane, Brixton; ///carry.latter.object**

Plonked between the hubbubs of Brixton, Herne Hill and Tulse Hill, Brockwell Park is a much, much-needed slice of greenery. Something is always afoot in the vast expanse of green, whether it's a Saturday Park Run, a basketball tournament or an alfresco birthday party. Come July, the Lambeth Country Show moves in for a weekend of animal displays, music performances and vegetable-growing competitions.

**» Don't leave without** visiting the hidden garden at Brockwell's western edge – it's a walled-off oasis with lots of quiet benches.

# PRIMROSE HILL

**Map 6; entrance via Primrose Hill Road, Primrose Hill; ///hook.sand.keys**

A hot contender for London's loveliest picnic spot, Primrose Hill rises up above the gastropubs, delis and cafés of Regent's Park Road, offering a cracking view of the city. In summer, its gentle incline is dotted with sunbathers and gaggles of friends; in autumn, locals huddle on the

Sunrise is the best time to admire the view from atop Primrose Hill —and you'll have it all to yourself.

slope to watch fireworks blaze across the skyline on Guy Fawkes night. And when winter sees snow, makeshift sledges miraculously appear overnight.

# CRYSTAL PALACE PARK

**Map 6; entrance via Thicket Road, Crystal Palace; ///model.tried.fade; www.crystalpalacepark.org.uk**

Crystal Palace residents will proudly point out that this isn't your average patch of grass. For one, this former Victorian Pleasure Ground survived the fire that destroyed the eponymous Crystal Palace. What they really love to talk about, though, are the dinosaurs. Strangely lumpy, quirky remnants of Victoriana, these concrete sculptures were the world's first life-size dinosaur replicas and have become beloved mascots of this area. If you're more about puzzles than prehistoric creatures, there's a maze that dates back to 1870.

Stroll through South London's little-known Sydenham Hill Woods and you'll forget you're in London. Through the wild undergrowth you can follow the trundling tracks of an abandoned railway line that served Crystal Palace until the 1950s and seek out the pretty Victorian folly. As you leave, don't miss the sweeping city views outside the Dulwich and Sydenham Golf Club, near the hidden wood's exit.

# On the Water

*For all its concrete and brick, London is a city shaped around water – river buses shuttle commuters along the Thames, rowing boats criss-cross the Serpentine and walkers stomp alongside willowy canals.*

## PADDLEBOARD ON REGENT'S CANAL

**Map 1; start at the Pirate Castle, Oval Road, Camden; ///people.weds.bets**

Okay, SUPing might seem better paired with the golden beaches of California than Britain's concrete capital. But paddleboarding has caught on here too and Regent's Canal is the place to do it. The stretch between Camden and Little Venice is particularly picturesque. Work your core as you paddle past the residents of London Zoo and river dwellers tending to their canal boat roof gardens.

## SIGHTSEE ABOARD THE THAMES CLIPPER

**Map 4; start at Putney Pier; ///gladiators.cure.cubs; www.thamesclippers.com**

London's smuggest commuters get the boat to work. The glorious city vistas, on-board coffee and guaranteed seats are a far cry from the cramped friction of rush hour on the Tube. It's a great way to get

Hop on the Clipper for the half-hour ride between Tate Britain and the Tate Modern; you can rest your feet and enjoy the views.

about – the river bus zips between 23 piers, giving you a front-row view of some of the capital's best landmarks for a few pounds. Make a day of it by starting in Putney and disembarking in Greenwich.

## FOLLOW THE WANDLE TRAIL

**Map 6; start at Carshalton Ponds, Carshalton; ///summer.scared.work; www.wandlevalleypark.co.uk**

A lot of Londoners haven't even heard of the River Wandle, which snakes through South London. Cyclists who have, however, spend their Saturdays following this 14-km (9-mile) route as it meanders through a clutch of parks that line the watercourse. Begin at Carshalton Ponds or, if you just fancy a taster, pick it up at Wimbledon Park.

**» Don't leave without** sinking a frothy pint at appropriately named pub The Wandle, just by Earlsfield train station.

## WALK THE THAMES PATH

**Map 4; start from Putney Pier; ///drift.glee.quit; www.thames-path.org.uk**

The River Thames is the very heart of London and every local has enjoyed a long walk along the Thames Path – it's the perfect way to blow away the cobwebs. Start in Putney, where rowing clubhouses line the riverbanks, and stroll towards Teddington, then follow the gravelly track that winds along the water's edge all the way to elegant Richmond. Tuck into a slap-up dinner at one of the gastropubs here before jumping on a train back to the city.

# Solo, Pair, Crowd

**Whether you're travelling alone, in a duo or en masse, there's a watery adventure to fit every gathering.**

## FLYING SOLO
### Water and wheels
See the city from two wheels by hiring a bike and cycling along the Regent's Canal towpath. Begin east in Victoria Park and pedal west, concluding in charming Little Venice, where you can enjoy a congratulatory waterside drink.

## IN A PAIR
### A boat for two on the Serpentine
Grab your best mate, or a family member, and a few provisions and take a rowing boat or pedalo across the serene waters of the Serpentine in Hyde Park.

## FOR A CROWD
### Party on a boat
Bring a blowout picnic and all your squad to board the beautiful *Jenny Wren* as it navigates Regent's Canal (*www.walkersquay.com*).

## WALTHAMSTOW WETLANDS

**Map 6; 2 Forest Road, Walthamstow; ///combining.share.food;**
**www.walthamstowwetlands.com;**

The long-standing domain of rare wildfowl, Europe's largest urban wetlands were opened to the public in 2017. Today the reservoirs don't just attract anglers and birders. Couples stroll hand in hand along the boardwalks, families enjoy leisurely picnics and mates cycle along the paths en route to Walthamstow's craft breweries.

**» Don't leave without** checking out the Wetlands Contemporary art programme at the Engine House, by the wetlands' entrance.

## WATERBUS RIDES TO CAMDEN

**Map 4; start at Warwick Crescent, Little Venice; ///pulse.onion.envy;**
**www.londonwaterbus.com**

Looking for date inspiration? This cutesy canalboat trundles up and down arguably the prettiest part of Regent's Canal. Embark at Little Venice and chug along to buzzy Camden Lock. Jump off here before tucking into snacks at eco-focused Buck Street Market.

## MUDLARKING ON THE NORTH BANK

**Map 2; access via the Trig Lane Stairs, North Bank; ///seats.sizes.clear;**
**www.thames-explorer.org.uk**

The tidal waters of the Thames churn up remnants of the past, with low tide unveiling time-lost detritus. Join a guide (safety first, remember) and a friendly community of mudlarkers to beachcomb for lost treasures; it will give you new insight into the city.

# Cemetery Strolls

*We know, it sounds odd, but London's gorgeous cemetery grounds – especially the so-called "Magnificent Seven" – are ideal for an afternoon's ramble or a simple bit of R & R.*

## ABNEY PARK CEMETERY

**Map 3; 215 Stoke Newington High Street, Stoke Newington;**
**///sung.animal.bigger; www.abneypark.org**

Wild and woody Abney Park Cemetery, perhaps most famous for featuring in the music video for Amy Winehouse's "Back to Black", is a great place to walk off brunch in the company of Stokey's past residents. Look for the graves of rebels, panto actors and a chap who taught the Victorians all about African and Asian wildlife – essentially the 19th-century David Attenborough (the lion on his grave is the clue).

## HIGHGATE CEMETERY

**Map 6; Swain's Lane, Highgate; ///audio.regard.scrap;**
**www.highgatecemetery.org**

It's hard to resist the grand allure of Highgate, with its towering monuments and statues. This is the final resting place of some big names; Karl Marx, George Eliot and Douglas Adams are all buried here, plus Alexander Litvinenko, who is buried in a lead coffin to prevent radioactive leaking. Join an organized tour on a Wednesday to learn more about other residents and how the Victorians were generally obsessed with death, which explains why London has all of these epic cemeteries littered with elaborate crypts.

**»** **Don't leave without** paying your respects at the grave of suffragist Ernestine Rose, who is dubbed "the first Jewish feminist".

## KENSAL GREEN CEMETERY

**Map 4; Harrow Road, Kensal Green; ///rooms.insist.tight;**
**www.kensalgreencemetery.com**

One of the oldest of the Magnificent Seven, Kensal Green Cemetery certainly has a Gothic noire quality about it. Horror films have been shot here and, in real life, the grounds have experienced some weird goings-on, including one poor pallbearer being killed by a coffin he was carrying. All this aside, the cemetery is an area of conservation and home to more than 30 species of bird, who break the eerie silence with their cheerful song.

## BUNHILL FIELDS BURIAL GROUND

**Map 2; 38 City Road, Old Street; ///gained.second.hurry; 020 7374 4127**

Grab a latte at nearby Workshop Coffee and take a turn around Bunhill Fields. It's not one of London's most famous, but it's easy to see why city slickers choose to eat their lunch in the company of Daniel Defoe and William Blake. This square of calming green offers genuine respite from the frenetic pace of central London.

## WANDSWORTH CEMETERY

**Map 6; 32 Magdalen Road, Wandsworth; ///wiping.remark.limes;**
**www.wandsworth.gov.uk**

Okay, it's not as grand other London cemeteries, so why visit Wandsworth Cemetery? Aside from the pretty and perfectly manicured grounds, the cemetery's views out over South London are hard to beat. And while an onslaught of joggers, families and raucous 20-somethings descend on nearby Wandsworth Common, you'll have the cemetery all to yourself.

## NUNHEAD CEMETERY

**Map 5; Linden Grove, Nunhead; ///slim.forest.preoccupied; www.fonc.org.uk**

This is the biggest of the Magnificent Seven and it's also the grandest. Tree-lined walkways sweep around its grounds, which are punctuated with huge tombs, monuments and the beautiful ruins of

**Shh!**

Many don't realize that down the road from Mile End Park and Victoria Park is Tower Hamlets Cemetery. You might mistake it for a spit of woodland, being as wild and unkept as it is; graves vie for space with flora and fauna and tree roots break up headstones. The East End was historically the city's poorest quarter and this is the graveyard of its ordinary people — around 350,000 residents in total. Wander the winding paths and, if you're not squeamish, forage the fertile ground for wild garlic.

an Anglican chapel. Speaking of grandeur, on the cemetery's western side you'll get a wonderful vista including St Paul's Cathedral and, on a clear day, beloved venue Alexandra Palace on the horizon. The groundsmen are even considerate enough to trim the trees to allow for an uninterrupted view.

## BROCKLEY CEMETERY

**Map 5; Ivy Road, Deptford; ///shot.manage.spits; www.foblc.org.uk**

As mentioned, the Victorians loved the macabre so they were naturally fascinated by Brockley Cemetery, where poisoner Amelia Winters was buried not far from murdered teen Jane Maria Clouson. Grim, but the grounds remain a pleasant place for a walk followed by a cheering drink at the London Beer Dispensary just down the road.

**» Don't leave without** visiting the adjacent Ladywell Cemetery, which opened within a month of its sister.

## BROMPTON CEMETERY

**Map 4; Fulham Road, Kensington; ///labs.lively.castle;**
**www.brompton-cemetery.org.uk**

Locals call Brompton the Cemetery of Light and Sun because both the inventors of sunglasses and traffic lights are buried here. And a walk here is especially lovely on a mellow summer or autumn day, when a golden light is cast across the grounds. Search for the grave of suffragette Emmeline Pankhurst and socialite Hannah Courtoy's tomb (which the Victorians believed was a time machine – weird) before concluding with a coffee in the cemetery's Café North Lodge.

# Community Gardens and Urban Farms

*Volunteer-led gardens and urban farms are a little-known side to London. Escape the heaving metropolis and get your hands dirty with the locals at one of these little rural outposts.*

## THE STORY GARDEN

**Map 1; Ossulston Street, Kings Cross; ///salon.down.lonely; www.globalgeneration.org.uk**

This community garden, grown in upcycled skips, has transformed a plot of land behind the Barbican Library. The Story Garden is a sustainable urban oasis built by and for the locals; a place to grow herbs and veg, and escape the furore of the city.

## PHYTOLOGY MEDICINAL GARDEN

**Map 2; Bethnal Green Nature Reserve, Middleton Street, Bethnal Green; ///usage.glue.codes; www.phytology.org.uk**

Puffs of yellow dandelions, dense clumps of nettles and dainty chamomile are grown in abundance on this transformed World War II bombsite. Set amid the woodland of Bethnal Green Nature

Reserve, this apothecary garden celebrates the medicinal power of the humble weed. And the community vibes are palpable. Stop by and an expert gardener in overalls will diagnose your latest ailment and point you in the direction of the plant to pick.

## SURREY DOCKS FARM

**Map 5; Rotherhithe Street, Surrey Quays; ///silly.walks.handy;**
**www.surreydocksfarm.org.uk**

While stressed bankers in suits pound the floors of Canary Wharf's skyscrapers, a blacksmith in old-fashioned garb hammers red-hot slabs of metal on Surrey Docks Farm. This farm is incongruous but it's a welcome slice of rural life. Local schoolkids learn about the city's farming history, creatives partake in ceramic classes and couples stock up on seasonal veg in the farm shop.

## VAUXHALL CITY FARM

**Map 5; 165 Tyers Street, Vauxhall; ///pram.entertainer.woes;**
**www.vauxhallcityfarm.org**

An afternoon spent on this central city farm might involve sheep-shearing demos or a chance to feed the chickens. But donate on arrival and know that your visit means much more besides. Vauxhall is a low-income area where opportunities for young people can be scarce. The farm responds to that with outreach and development programmes that reach 7,000 children every year.

**» Don't leave without** popping into the nearby Tea House Theatre, which serves refreshing loose-leaf teas and slabs of homemade cake.

# DALSTON EASTERN CURVE GARDEN

**Map 3; Dalston Lane, Hackney; ///hobby.ladder.wiped;**
**www.dalstongarden.org**

A social enterprise since 2012, Dalston's eco garden – built on an old railway track – is an oasis. Bees drift from herb to flower and groups of friends catch up on tree stumps in the fairy-lit garden, usually to the soundtrack of someone strumming a guitar.

# HACKNEY CITY FARM

**Map 2; 1A Goldsmiths Row, Hackney; ///global.spin.flag;**
**www.hackneycityfarm.co.uk**

Almost entirely run by volunteers, Hackney City Farm is all about community. Green-fingered locals pitch in with the garden, 30-somethings in hand-knitted jumpers pick up produce and kids make friends with the animals. Come for weekend brunch at its café and you'll be offering to harvest some veg before you know it.

**»** **Don't leave without** buying a pot of their home-produced honey. It's so good that you're only allowed two jars per person.

# CULPEPER COMMUNITY GARDEN

**Map 1; 1 Cloudesley Road, Angel; ///foster.chops.custom;**
**www.culpeper.org.uk**

Local volunteers from all backgrounds tend to this wonderful garden, hidden by high walls, and each puts their own personal stamp on the flowery scene. They'll most likely be pouring a cuppa in the tea hut as you arrive; join them before a tour.

## Liked by the locals

"Both nature and people flourish in community gardens. They are London's mini havens, where we can connect with others and with the earth; there's nothing more satisfying than having a cup of freshly picked mint tea after working together in the garden."

ABI JOHNSTON, CLINICAL SCIENTIST AND BROCKWELL PARK COMMUNITY GARDEN VOLUNTEER

# Nearby Getaways

*Of course Londoners love their city but sometimes a change of scene and gulp of fresh air are just what the doctor ordered. Luckily the capital has various tempting day trips in easy reach.*

## EPPING FOREST

### 1-hour Tube from Oxford Circus

Wedged between London and the county of Essex, this ancient woodland feels worlds away from the hubbub of the Big Smoke. So, come the weekend, those craving the great outdoors don their walking boots and set off on a hike along the sun-dappled forest floor, stopping to picnic by one of the ponds that punctuate the landscape and concluding their walk with a reviving pint in one of Epping's cosy pubs. Pure bliss.

# BRIGHTON

**1-hour train from Victoria station or 1.5 hour train from St Pancras International station; www.visitbrighton.com**

Pebbly beaches dotted with optimistic sun-soakers, jaunty fairground rides and chirpy ice cream vans: for classic British seaside charms, Brighton ticks all the boxes. But many Londoners skip the beach entirely. After all, there are bargains to pick up in the Lanes' vintage shops, coffees to drink at independent roasters and a sustainably focused food scene to sample. All this in the most friendly and inclusive of communities. What more could you want?

**>> Don't leave without** renting a bike from one of the city's public docking stations and cycling along the seafront to nearby Hove, Brighton's chilled out next-door neighbour.

# MARGATE

**1.5-hour train from St Pancras International station; www.visitthanet.co.uk**

Margate is the go-to coastal hotspot for hipster, arty types (hence the nickname Shoreditch-on-sea). Day-trippers come for a blast of salty-aired nostalgia, to browse the vintage shops and check out the Turner Contemporary. Margate may have experienced gentrification – there are craft beer, natural wine and independent coffee places galore – but it's kept its edge. Check out the retro rides at Dreamland for proof.

# RYE

**1-hour train from St Pancras International station**

City slickers descend on Rye on their days off. And who can blame them? This hilltop town in East Sussex is pure charm, with its cobbled lanes, antique shops, wonky pubs and pretty harbour. Better still, the golden dunes of Camber Sands are a 5-km (3-mile) stroll away – perfect for walking off a slap-up meal of fish and chips.

**» Don't leave without** ordering a scoop or two from Mermaid Street Café's ice cream window before walking up pretty Mermaid Street.

# CAMBRIDGE

**1.5-hour train from Kings Cross or Liverpool Street stations**

Picture this: medieval streets thronging with students cycling to lectures, a river peppered with punting parties, crooked tea houses abuzz with chatter. Welcome to Cambridge, rival to the university city that-shall-not-be-named. This is the day trip Londoners roll out when they want to feel a bit more refined – a day out with the in-laws or a classy escape with the girls. Its magical charm never disappoints.

## Try it!
## GO PUNTING

Sure, you can pay someone to chauffeur you down the River Cam. But it's way more fun to impress your friends with your own punting skills. Book onto a lesson with a Scudamore's expert (*www.scudamores.com*).

# THE CHILTERNS

### 30-minute train from Marylebone station or 1-hour Tube from Euston Square; www.visitchilterns.co.uk

Zip along on a train or Tube to the historic town of Amersham, the gateway to the beautiful Chilterns. Enjoy a riverside walk along the River Misbourne on arrival, pausing for lunch at one of the inviting pubs (perhaps The Swan, which has a lovely big garden and a great vegan menu). Then it's time for another dose of bracing fresh air with a country stroll in the surrounding Chiltern Hills. Lovely stuff.

# BRISTOL

### 1.5-hour train from Paddington station; www.visitbristol.co.uk

If Londoners could live in another UK city, they would choose Bristol – this city is a hotbed for creativity, with cool start-ups popping up left, right and centre. And just think, if you did move, you could have all this: the street-art splashed streets of Stokes Croft, the view of ice-cream-hued houses teetering up the hills above the waterfront, the drama of the Clifton Suspension Bridge and the shipping container foodie hotspot of Wapping Wharf.

# WHITSTABLE

### 1.5-hour train from Victoria or Cannon Street stations

Yes, this seaside town is a looker – boats bob out at sea, there are pastel-hued beach huts and atmospheric lanes – but it's the seafood that visitors have their eye on. A pint at the beachside Old Neptune is a must, as is getting oysters shucked right in front of you at The Forge.

HAMPSTEAD LANE

## Stretch your legs on
## HAMPSTEAD HEATH

Walk off your lunch in this huge expanse of greenery. If you're feeling brave, why not take a dip in one of the ponds?

**5**

## Tuck into lunch at
## SPANIARDS INN

**4**

This charming pub is always abuzz with families and dog-walkers. Make for the lovely, leafy beer garden, which has plenty of seats – the perfect setting for a hearty roast.

SPANIARDS ROAD

MERTON LANE

HIGHGATE

WEST HILL

*Hampstead Heath*

## Mooch around
## HAMPSTEAD VILLAGE

Wander through the cobbled streets and stop to window-shop at the antiques shops, fashion boutiques and florists.

EAST HEATH RD

**3**

## Enjoy the view from
## PARLIAMENT HILL
## VIEWPOINT

After climbing Parliament Hill, take a breather and drink in the incredible city scenery from the summit.

**2**  HAMPSTEAD

HAMPSTEAD HIGH ST

DOWNSHIRE HILL

MANSFIELD ROAD

**1**

## Grab coffee at
## GINGER AND WHITE

Start with a flat white and slice of carrot cake at one of the pavement tables at this café, tucked away in a pretty mews.

*Romantic poet John Keats lived at* **Keats House** *between 1818 and 1820. Here he fell in love with Fanny Brawne, who lived opposite.*

**GOSPEL OAK**

# A day in
# idyllic Hampstead

Hampstead has it all: gorgeous old mansions, characterful pubs, fashionable boutiques and – the jewel in its crown – wild, undulating heathland. Long characterized by its intellectual, artistic, musical and literary residents, the north London neighbourhood is rich with history. Come the weekend, Londoners love nothing more than a stroll around Hampstead village and heath, fantasizing about their dream house and sighing over its picture-postcard scenery.

**HIGHGATE**

**HIGHGATE HILL**

**SWAIN'S LANE**

**6 Snoop around HIGHGATE CEMETERY**
Wild and overgrown, this graveyard holds some famous remains; look out for the graves of poet Christina Rossetti and philosopher and socialist Karl Marx.

**KESHOTT AVENUE**

**DARTMOUTH PARK HILL**

**TUFNELL PARK**

**HIGHGATE ROAD**

**1. Ginger and White**
4a–5a Perrin's Court;
www.gingerandwhite.com;
///tricky.dark.author

**2. Hampstead Village**
Hampstead High Street;
www.hampsteadvillage
london.com;
///cable.scuba.spicy

**3. Parliament Hill Viewpoint**
Hampstead Heath;
///tower.defeat.land

**4. Spaniards Inn**
Spaniards Road;
www.thespaniards
hampstead.co.uk;
///envy.logs.engine

**5. Hampstead Heath**
www.hampsteadheath.net;
///fakes.prime.album

**6. Highgate Cemetery**
Swain's Lane, Highgate;
www.highgatecemetery.org;
///audio.regard.scrap

Keats House ///hangs.booth.humans

189

*With a little research and preparation, this city will feel like a home away from home. Check out these websites to ensure a healthy, safe stay in London.*

# London
## DIRECTORY

## SAFE SPACES

London is a diverse and inclusive city, but should you feel uneasy at any point or want to find your community, there are spaces catering to different genders, sexualities, demographics and religions.

### www.blackownedlondon.com

*A curated online guide to London's Black-owned businesses.*

### www.jw3.org.uk

*An all-encompassing cultural centre for London's Jewish communities.*

### www.londonmandir.baps.org

*A Hindu temple acting as a welcoming cultural centre for all.*

### www.muslimsinbritain.org

*The definitive guide to mosques and Muslim community spaces in the UK.*

### www.stonewall.org.uk

*Charity offering support for the LGBTQ+ community, as well as a list of services and groups in your area.*

### www.switchboard.lgbt

*An LGBTQ+ helpline to talk through any problems and find support among like-minded people.*

## HEALTH

The UK's National Health Service, the NHS, provides free emergency care for all, regardless of their nationality. Non-emergency care is usually not free, however, so make sure you take out comprehensive health insurance before you visit.

### www.babylonhealth.com

*Talk to a doctor or check your symptoms online via this NHS-affiliated service.*

**www.boots-uk.com**
*UK's leading pharmacy-led retailer with a Midnight Pharmacy service at 60 of its shops around London.*

**www.citizenaid.org**
*A resource full of first-aid tips.*

**www.guysandstthomas.nhs.uk**
*An A&E department and walk-in urgent care centre across the river from Big Ben.*

**www.homerton.nhs.uk/sexual-health**
*Walk-in sexual health clinic at Clifden Centre, Homerton University Hospital.*

**www.nhs.uk**
*The UK healthcare system's website, full of advice and a list of health centres.*

## TRAVEL SAFETY ADVICE
London is a relatively safe city. Before you travel – and while you're here – always keep tabs on the latest UK regulations.

**www.met.police.uk**
*Information about major police incidents in the city.*

**www.relayuk.bt.com**
*App that helps those who are hearing- or speech-impaired contact 999 (emergency services) via SMS.*

**www.report-it.org.uk**
*A website for reporting hate crimes, with a list of organizations that can help victims.*

**www.visitlondon.com/coronavirus**
*The latest coronavirus-related news in London, directly from the government.*

## ACCESSIBILITY
London is ranked as one of Europe's most accessible cities for anyone with mobility concerns. These resources will help make your journeys go smoothly.

**www.euansguide.com**
*A forum for disabled access reviews on restaurants, theatres and attractions, by and for people with specific requirements.*

**www.scope.org.uk**
*Charity providing advice and support on how to get help on public transport.*

**www.tfl.gov.uk/transport-accessibility**
*Transport for London's official website with an accessible journey planner and up-to-date news on step-free station access.*

**www.visitlondon.com**
*London's official visitor guide with an Accessible London section, jam-packed with recommendations on accessible hotels, tours and attractions.*

## ABOUT THE ILLUSTRATOR

### Mantas Tumosa

*Creative designer and illustrator Mantas moved from his home country of Lithuania to London back in 2011. By day, he's busy creating bold, minimalistic illustrations that tell a story – such as the gorgeous cover of this book. By night, he's dreaming of adventures away, catching up on the basketball and cooking Italian food (which he can't get enough of).*

**Main Contributors** Florence Derrick, Marlene Landu, Olivia Pass

**Senior Editor** Lucy Richards

**Senior Designer** Tania Gomes

**Project Editor** Zoë Rutland

**Project Art Editor** Bharti Karakoti

**Editors** Elsepth Beidas, Lucy Sara-Kelly

**Proofreader** Stephanie Smith

**Senior Cartographic Editor** Casper Morris

**Jacket Designer** Tania Gomes

**Jacket Illustrator** Mantas Tumosa

**Senior Production Editor** Jason Little

**Senior Production Controller** Stephanie McConnell

**Managing Editor** Hollie Teague

**Managing Art Editor** Bess Daly

**Art Director** Maxine Pedliham

**Publishing Director** Georgina Dee

First edition 2021

Published in Great Britain by Dorling Kindersley Limited, DK, One Embassy Gardens, 8 Viaduct Gardens, London SW11 7BW.

The authorised representative in the EEA is Dorling Kindersley Verlag GmbH. Arnulfstr. 124, 80636 Munich, Germany.

Published in the United States by DK Publishing, 1450 Broadway, Suite 801, New York, NY 10018.

Copyright © 2021 Dorling Kindersley Limited
A Penguin Random House Company
21 22 23 24 10 9 8 7 6 5 4 3 2

A CIP catalog record for this book is available from the British Library.

A catalog record for this book is available from the Library of Congress.

ISSN: 1542 1554
ISBN: 978 0 2414 9068 6

Printed and bound in Canada.

www.dk.com

### A NOTE FROM DK EYEWITNESS

The world is fast-changing and it's keeping us folk at DK Eyewitness on our toes. We've worked hard to ensure that this edition of London Like a Local is up-to-date and reflects today's favourite places but we know that standards shift, venues close and new ones pop up in their place. So, if you notice something has closed, we've got something wrong or left something out, we want to hear about it. Please drop us a line at travelguides@dk.com